Maje

Experiencing Authentic Worship

S. JOSEPH KIDDER

With love + blessings.
May God surround you
with His presence, love
+ grace.

Joe + Denise
Kidder
Rm 8:28

R

REVIEW AND HERALD® PUBLISHING ASSOCIATION

Since 1861 | www.reviewandherald.com

DEDICATION

To Denise,
my beloved wife.
Your worship experience is
inspiring and contagious.

Published by Review and Herald® Publishing Association, Hagerstown, MD 21741-1119

Review and Herald® titles may be purchased in bulk for educational, business, fund-raising, or sales promotional use. For information, e-mail SpecialMarkets@reviewandherald.com.

The Review and Herald® Publishing Association publishes biblically based materials for spiritual, physical, and mental growth and Christian discipleship.

The author assumes full responsibility for the accuracy of all facts and quotations as cited in this book.

Scripture quotations marked NASB are from the *New American Standard Bible,* copyright © 1960, 1962, 1963, 1968, 1971, 1972, 1973, 1975, 1977, 1994 by The Lockman Foundation. Used by permission.

Texts credited to NIV are from the *Holy Bible, New International Version.* Copyright © 1973, 1978, 1984, International Bible Society. Used by permission of Zondervan Bible Publishers.

Texts credited to NKJV are from the New King James Version. Copyright © 1979, 1980, 1982 by Thomas Nelson, Inc. Used by permission. All rights reserved.

This book was
Edited by Gerald Wheeler
Copyedited by James Cavil
Cover designed by Trent Truman
Interior designed by Tina M. Ivany
Cover art by © istock.com: Richmatts (clouds), Alex Bond (scroll)
Typeset: Bembo 11/14

PRINTED IN U.S.A.

13   12   11   10   09   5   4   3   2   1

Library of Congress Cataloging-in-Publication Data

Kidder, Joe, 1953-   .
   Majesty : experiencing authentic worship / Joe Kidder.
        p. cm.
   1. Worship—Biblical teaching. 2. Worship. I. Title.
   BS680.W78K53 2009
   248.3—dc22

                                              2008049319

ISBN 978-0-8280-2423-5

CONTENTS

Chapter 1   Worship: The Heartbeat of the Believer.........................7

Chapter 2   What Is Worship?.......................................17

Chapter 3   A Biblical Model of Worship 26

Chapter 4   How to Behave in a Worshipful Way..........................33

Chapter 5   Prayer and Worship 47

Chapter 6   The Word of God and Worship 57

Chapter 7   Praise and Worship.......................................68

Chapter 8   Offering and Worship................................77

Chapter 9   The Church of My Dreams 87

Chapter 10   The Thrill of Worship 101

"The twenty-four elders will fall down before Him
who sits on the throne, and will worship Him
who lives forever and ever, and will cast
their crowns before the throne, saying,
'Worthy are You, our Lord and our God,
to receive glory and honor and power;
for You created all things, and because of Your
will they existed, and were created"
(Rev. 4:10, 11, NASB).

1

WORSHIP
The Heartbeat of the Believer

WHAT IS WORSHIP?

It was a cold winter evening in the Northwest. About 200 people had assembled for our church vision night. God had blessed our congregation in an awesome way, as more than 100 people had joined our church that year. Many great and wonderful things had happened in our lives, community, and congregation. The level of excitement was high. You could feel joy and warmth everywhere.

I started my devotional thought by saying that we were here to worship and to praise the Lord for all the wonderful things that He had done. Then I continued by asking the question "What is worship?"

Some thought that listening to a sermon was worship, while others decided that evangelism was worship. Some equated it with revival, and others suggested that believing or teaching the truth was worship. Of course, some believed that worship was about praise and adoration. Many expressed the opinion that offering, fellowship, and even prayer were preliminaries to worship, but not the real worship itself. No one mentioned that worship was about God, about making a commitment to Him and giving Him worth, honor, glory, and devotion.

Almost everyone put the emphasis on what happens up front on Sabbath morning, forgetting that worship is about life and what takes place inside of us every moment of every day.

WHAT IS YOUR EXPERIENCE OF WORSHIP?

It seems to me that very few Christians know much about true worship. Most Christians in most churches have little knowledge of worship and even less of an experience in actual worship of God. We go to church, but we don't worship. We sing songs, but we don't worship. And we listen to sermons, but we don't worship. All of these things are elements of worship, but they are not worship. You can do all of them and yet have truly failed to worship God. We Christians often mistake the means of worship for worship itself.

Worship, though many believe this, is not about us being in church during the 11:00 service on Sabbath morning. No, worship is not about us showing up, but about God showing up and breaking through inside of us and bringing His presence and grace to us. It is about being caught up in the majesty and wonder and awe of God. At its core, worship is about being so moved by the presence of God that we kneel down in obedience and devotion and then rise up in holy lives filled with service and excitement for what God has done and is doing for us.

After that discussion about worship, I immediately felt the need for a comprehensive program of education to explain to the congregation its meaning and essential elements. I believed that proper understanding of worship and the implementation of meaningful worship services would create excitement and enhance spirituality. And the results were amazing. The more I explained to the congregation the significance of worship, the more satisfaction I found among the members and the more they were inclined to do ministry and evangelism. When we enter into an authentic experience with our awesome God, we are more likely to live His will in the world and serve Him with love and enthusiasm.

I also believe there is a strong connection between personal worship and congregational worship. One leads to the other. If one is weak, the other will also eventually be weak. However, if one is strong, it will inevitably make the other strong.

I believe that as you read this book your understanding of worship will deepen, heightening its experience for you.

WHY AUTHENTIC WORSHIP?

Worship is the single most important event in the life of the Christian, for everything in Christianity centers on worship. The health and vitality of the believer rises and falls on the quality of his or her worship experience. Worship, according to Revelation 14:6-12, is the commemoration of Creation and the celebration of the gospel. It is the believer's response to the mercy and goodness of God through the act of adoration, reverence, thanksgiving, obedience, and submission.

Christians worship because of what God has done, is doing, and will do through His Son, Jesus Christ, and through His Spirit. The chief aim of Christian worship is to glorify God, to praise Him, and to thank Him—to enter into a definite experience with Him. Therefore, worship is one of the most important activities of the believer and the church. If the church fails in its worship, it will also stumble in its mission and degenerate into nothing but a social club with some spiritual bent.

In order to improve our spiritual activities and mission, we must have a proper understanding of worship. Without authentic worship, spiritual life would soon weaken and disintegrate. There can be no possibility for us as believers of being healthy and strong spiritually without worship.

Recognizing, then, that Christian worship is the essential issue in the life of the Christian believer and that an understanding of it is long overdue, the following chapters will attempt to come to grips with the concept of worship.

The purpose of this book is to introduce and explain the scriptural principles of Christian worship. I believe that the more we comprehend worship and the significance of its elements, the more worship will become meaningful and eventually lead to a higher commitment to Jesus and to His ministry and mission.

THE LIFE YOU HAVE ALWAYS WANTED

The Christian life centers on worship. However, a failure to grasp the proper meaning of worship leads to frustration, confusion, and decline in spirituality. There is widespread ignorance about its true significance and basic elements (i.e., Scripture, preaching, prayer, praise, offering, and fellowship), and the means of attaining the blessing of rich, rewarding, authentic worship.

It is, therefore, not surprising that multitudes of people, both young and old, who in childhood worshipped at home and regularly attended church, have turned away from the Lord and the church, expressing their loss of interest and their failure to find meaning and relevance in personal as well as corporate worship.

Understanding and experiencing worship is essential for the following reasons:

First, true worship takes place when the individual believer seeks the Lord with all his or her heart, mind, soul, passion, and energy. Jeremiah declares, "For I know the plans that I have for you,' declares the Lord, 'plans for welfare and not for calamity to give you a future and a hope. Then you will call upon Me and come and pray to Me, and I will listen to you. You will seek Me and find Me when you search for Me with all your heart. I will be found by you,' declares the Lord, 'and I will restore your fortunes and will gather you from all the nations and from all the places where I have driven you,' declares the Lord" (Jer. 29:11-14, NASB).

Such passion for God will help us enter His presence and have an encounter that will change us and bring us into a higher level of commitment and love for Him. The believer must worship not so much to have his or her needs met, but to seek God more than life itself. The most common mistake that Christians make in worship today is seeking an experience rather than God Himself.

Unfortunately, Christians limit their worship to one hour each week. And when they come to that service, they often do so just to observe and be entertained. I have been at church services that opened with the following statement: "We want you to sit back, relax, and enjoy the program we have prepared for you."

We have reversed the whole concept of worship because we think that the pastor and worship leaders are the entertainers and we are the audience. But in true worship we are the performers, the pastors and worship leaders are the directors, and God is the audience. Because our concept of worship is backwards, we want to know what's in it for us. If we are truly going to worship, we must come to the realization that worship is not for us, but for God. Because God desires our worship, we must learn how to worship Him.

If we attempt to meet our needs, we will end up frustrated, disappointed, and dissatisfied, for we cannot fully satisfy them. But if we seek to meet God, it will fulfill our needs, because He is what our souls really desire.

Second, true worship focuses on God—the point at which many of us make our mistake. We assume that worship focuses on us. Many times I've heard people talk about how they are struggling in their worship life because they aren't being fed. Have you ever heard anyone say that? "I'm not being fed. I'm not getting anything out of worship. I'm not being nurtured by worship. I don't get a blessing out of worship." I want to see people being concerned about whether or not *God* is enjoying worship. And until He gets something out of our worship, we never will. Until our worship blesses Him, we won't be blessed.

All too often we treat worship as something that's supposed to entertain us. But it isn't. What is most important is that God enjoys the worship experience. We are here to worship and bless *Him*.

Isaiah 6:1-6 describes how the prophet went to the Temple in which he "saw the Lord seated on a throne, high and exalted, and the train of his robe filled the temple" (verse 1, NIV). It is God's presence that fills the worship. True worship always focuses on Him.

Third, true worship always begins with a recognition of divine holiness. The 24 elders in Revelation 4:10, 11 worshipped God continually when they became aware of His power and character. We've lost something of that in our worship services. In recent years theology and worship have emphasized the personal nature, love, and joy of God to such a degree that for some reason we've forgotten that He is also an awesome deity. In the process we have almost transformed Him into a "little buddy." As a result we have forgotten that God is such an awesome and holy being that to be in His presence is to be filled with awe and wonder.

When Moses sensed God's presence in the burning bush, he became afraid. As Jacob had his dream of the ladder to heaven, he declared, "Surely the Lord is present and I didn't know it" (see Gen. 28:16). And the Bible says that awe swept over him. Time and again, when people become aware of the divine presence, the Bible describes the experience as one filled with awe, reverence, and even fear (see Heb. 12:28).

Why do we worship God? Because He is holy, and His holiness demands our attention.

Fourth, true worship is our *attributing worth to God*. In Scripture worship refers to the response of God's people to the wonder of who He is. For example, in Romans 12:1 Paul writes, "Therefore, I urge you, brothers, in view of God's mercy, to offer your bodies as living sacrifices, holy and pleasing to God—*this is your spiritual act of worship*" (NIV). But most frequently when the Bible uses the word "worship" it has to do with praising God—verbally attributing worth to Him. How often do you attribute worth to God in your life, in your giving, in your ministry, and in your personal and community worship?

Fifth, true worship also helps us to understand ourselves and our shortcomings and to seek God's forgiveness. In Isaiah 6 the heavenly beings sing, "Holy, holy, holy is the Lord Almighty; the whole earth is full of his glory" (Isa. 6:3, NIV). And immediately the prophet cries out, "Woe to me!" (verse 5, NIV). And he speaks of his own sinfulness.

We cannot come into the presence of God without becoming aware of both God's holiness and our own ungodliness.

Paul, in his letter to the Romans, said, "All have sinned and fall short of the glory of God" (Rom. 3:23, NIV). It is impossible to approach His presence without recognizing our own shortcomings and sins.

When Isaiah enters the Temple and senses God's holiness, it compels him to acknowledge his own sinfulness and to confess his sins. That confession leads to the free forgiveness of sins. In the book of Isaiah a heavenly being symbolically takes a hot coal and touches the lips of the prophet as a gesture that declares his sins are forgiven.

First John 1:8, 9 declares: "If we say that we have no sin, we deceive ourselves, and the truth is not in us. If we confess our sins, He is faithful and just to forgive us our sins and to cleanse us from all unrighteousness" (NKJV).

Again, why do we worship? One reason is to be able to experience that forgiveness. We need to hear the same message the prophet Isaiah did: "Your guilt is taken away and your sin atoned for" (Isa. 6:7, NIV).

Sixth, true worship will always result in service. Another reason we come to worship is so that our lives will be different. And the difference should be in terms of transformation and service. Worship at its best always motivates the worshipper to live a holy and righteous life filled with service, ministry, and blessings.

In Matthew 4:10 "worship" and "service" are essentially the same word. Worship and service go hand in hand. One cannot have worship without service automatically following.

As the prophet Isaiah is in the Temple to worship he hears angels singing, "Holy, holy, holy." It moves him to confess his sins, and he immediately receives assurance of his pardon. Then God asks, "Whom shall I send? And who will go for us?" (Isa. 6:8, NIV). And what follows then is the service, the ministry, the reaching out to others. Isaiah declares, "Here am I. Send me!" (verse 8). True worship will always result in service. We cannot enter into the worship of the Almighty without afterward departing into the world to serve. Worship challenges us to do something to make a difference in the world.

The real question is What is God calling you to do this week? What person in your life must you love a little more? Which people in your community do you need to reach out to a little harder?

What God summons us to do from one week to the next may change, but may our response always be that of Isaiah's: "Here I am, Lord, send me."

Therefore, the stronger that our grasp becomes on the deeper meanings of Christian worship, the more we enter into a rehearsal of the drama of our salvation. It is imperative that we seek an intelligent understanding of what Christian worship is. Only then will we have a more fulfilling Christian experience.

God's Greatest Desire Is to Be With Us

I believe that a strong connection exists between feeling the presence of God and authentic worship. When Christ is present, worship comes alive. Going to church is no longer just a self-centered act—to see what we'll get out of a service. Formality without meaning will then cease as we stop going through the motions of religious experience without any real power. The "tradition" of singing hymns—words and melodies—without a companion inward change will disappear. As we feel the presence of God, we will have the worship experience of our lives—rich, and deep, and meaningful.

I remind you that our Lord *is* truly present in us in our lives and in His church Sabbath after Sabbath. And what does that say about our worship practices? It affirms for us that when we worship we are having an audience with the King of the whole universe.

If the president of the United States or the queen of England were special guests in our churches, people would hurry to fill the pews. So why don't we do the same when our Lord and Master is the honored guest?

Human beings have a longing that I believe stretches as far back as the paradise of Eden. It is the desire to experience once again the wonder of the divine presence.

This intimacy first manifested itself in the garden. But then Adam and Eve sinned, and the Bible records that instead of continuing to enjoy the divine closeness of their Lord, "The man and his wife hid themselves from the presence of God" (Gen. 3:8, NASB). From that initial point one can almost read Scripture as an account of repeated attempts by both the Creator and His creatures to restore the cherished relationship known at the start of human history.

This presence of the Lord is an important theme throughout the Bible. In Exodus 33:14 God promised Moses, "My Presence will go with you, and I will give you rest" (NIV). The Lord had already fulfilled the divine promise in a supernatural way: "And the Lord went before them by day in a pillar of cloud to lead them along the way, and by night in a pillar of fire to give them light" (Ex. 13:21, NKJV). God also displayed His unique presence in the tabernacle ("Then the cloud covered the Tent of Meeting, and the glory of the Lord filled the tabernacle" [Ex. 40:34, NIV]) and later in the Temple ("When Solomon finished praying, fire came down from heaven and consumed the burnt offering and the sacrifices, and the glory of the Lord filled the temple" [2 Chron. 7:1, NIV]).

On a more personal level, the psalmist declared, "In thy presence is fulness of joy!" (Ps. 16:11). What a great truth we find contained in David's simple statement.

Yet God, in His love, was preparing to make His presence known to His people in a far more personal way than He ever had before.

In the New Testament the Gospels record the fulfillment of the greatest manifestation of the presence of God. The angel told Mary, "The Holy Spirit will come upon you, and the power of the Most High will overshadow you. So the holy one to be born will be called the Son of God" (Luke 1:35, NIV). So the miracle of miracles happened when God took on flesh so that human beings could know His presence firsthand. "'The virgin will be with child and will give birth to a son, and they will call him Immanuel'—which means, 'God with us'" (Matt. 1:23, NIV, referring to Isa. 7:14).

When Christ ascended to heaven, the church would continue to know the divine presence through the Holy Spirit, who came at Pentecost and now empowers the church.

Think about it this way. God manifested His desire to be with us in all the major events in history.

Creation—God created us because He felt lonely and desired our company.

The Sabbath—it is the weekly date that we have with the lover of our soul.

The sanctuary—it is the symbol of God's presence among us.

Jesus Christ—He is Immanuel, God is with us.

The Holy Spirit—He is God with us today.

All that we can say is that God is madly in love with us and wants to be with us always.

The Second Coming—that is when we can be with Him forever. The difference between the Sabbath and the Second Coming is that on the Sabbath we meet Jesus through the eyes of faith, while at the Second Advent we will meet Him face to face.

Enter into the presence of God. Worship and adore Him.

OUR DEEPEST NEED IS TO BE WITH HIM

In September of 2004 President George W. Bush came to South Bend, Indiana, about 30 miles from where I live, for a fund-raiser. The South Bend *Tribune* mentioned that the Republican Party had rented a large auditorium for the occasion and had a special dinner and evening with the president. However, what caught my attention was the fact that to get into the auditorium and eat a plate of chicken and asparagus would cost about $30,000. And if you wanted to sit close to the president, that privilege went for $50,000. And should you desire to join the president at his table and have your picture taken with him, that would call for a mere $100,000. (It would be the most expensive chicken and asparagus you'd ever eat. I believe this would the equivalent of buying such a meal for the rest of your life.)

Well, I did not believe the accuracy of the article, but still was interested in the details. So I called the paper and asked them exactly what the dinner and photo opportunity would cost. They assured me that all the facts in the article were correct. Also they told me that all presidential candidates do the same type of fund-raising.

At that moment I felt really good. My heart started rejoicing, and I had one of the greatest worship experiences of my life.

I was struck with awe and amazement that the King of kings, the Lord of lords, and the President of the whole universe desires to be with me. He has called me to be with Him for free! I don't have to pay a penny for it. All that I have to do is accept His invitation and enjoy His presence and bask in His company. In Mark 3:14 we read that Jesus "appointed twelve, that they would be with Him and that He could send them out to preach, and to have authority to cast out the demons" (NASB). Jesus has called you to be with Him. Enter into the presence of God. Worship and love Him. Give yourself as a living sacrifice to Him.

As you read this book, I invite you to go with me on a journey to the heart of God to experience authentic worship and to be caught up in the wonder and majesty of our Lord and Creator and Savior, Jesus Christ.

I pray that as you read this book, your whole being will be filled with the presence of God and your heart will be warmed by His grace.

Worship Is an Encounter With God,
in Which Our Hearts Touch His Heart

"Worthy is the Lamb that was slain to receive power,
and riches, and wisdom, and strength, and honour,
and glory, and blessing" (Rev. 5:12).

John 4:4-26; Isa. 6:1-8; Acts 2:42-47

2

What Is Worship?

*I*n our family worship we were reading through the Bible. One day, after breakfast, I called the family together. Stephanie, my daughter, who was 8 years old at the time, looked at me and asked, "What is worship? How do you worship?"

I told her that worship is reading our Bible story and doing what Jesus tells us to do. Apparently, my answer did not strike a chord with her young mind. The following day she came to me and inquired again, "What is worship?" How would you have answered? "Well, that is what we do in church—kneeling, standing, and sitting. We have three times of kneeling, four songs, one or two prayers, one sermon, and oh, by the way, an offering." Or: "Worship is what we do at home when we read the Bible and pray whether alone or with others."

Ponder the phrase word "worship experience." Is your reaction "Oh, that's Sabbath morning at 11:00"? Perhaps for some people the phrase worship experience serves only as a means to distinguish the Sabbath morning service from Sabbath evening vespers or from the Wednesday evening prayer meeting.

Does the phrase "worship experience" make you think of preaching or Communion? of singing or prayer? of praising or meditating? I believe that most of us regard the sermon as the essence of worship, or at least the main ingredient. Everything else is just preliminary.

Whatever else the word "worship" suggests to you, it should speak mainly about our responses to God. A worship experience does not take place just because you decide on a certain time for it to happen. Worship is an encounter with God. It happens when our hearts touch the heart of God. Worship occurs when we feel the touch of God. Worship is finding ourselves engulfed with the grace, mercy, and warmth of God's presence. Thus worship can take place anytime, anywhere, under any circumstance, when we meet God and desire to be changed by Him. Some worship experiences I can put beforehand in my calendar. But then I have had some very powerful and unexpected moments, during which I have felt the touch and warmth of the heart of God. Amazingly, they came while I was driving, jogging, reading, or even talking to someone. I also have felt them at home or in my office, in the church, or at a park. They could come when I was doing great, as well as when I was stressed; when I was happy, and when I was in the dumps. God is everywhere and always present.

A worship experience does not happen merely because we have labeled a certain time period in the church schedule of events as one. It is likely that we have all found ourselves in a "worship experience" in which, by appearance at least, there seemed to be little true worshipping of God.

A story I read some time ago illustrates this point. After attending church with his father one Sabbath morning, a little boy, before getting into bed that evening, knelt at his bedside and prayed, "Dear God, we had a good time at church today, but I wish You had been there." You could be at home or in church even praying or singing or reading the Bible and still not be worshipping.

What, then, is worship? Listen to what the psalmist says:

"Praise the Lord, O my soul; all my inmost being, praise his holy name.

Praise the Lord, O my soul, and forget not all his benefits—who forgives all your sins and heals all your diseases, who redeems your life from the pit and crowns you with love and compassion, who satisfies your desires with good things so that your youth is renewed like the eagle's. The Lord works righteousness and justice for all the oppressed" (Ps. 103:1-6, NIV).

The prophet Samuel declared: "Now then, stand here, because I am going to confront you with evidence before the Lord as to all the righteous acts performed by the Lord for you and your fathers" (1 Sam. 12:7, NIV).

Next read the exaltation of the Lamb as an example of authentic and powerful worship:

"'You are worthy to take the scroll and to open its seals, because you were slain, and with your blood you purchased men for God from every tribe and language and people and nation.' . . . 'Worthy is the Lamb, who was slain, to receive power and wealth and wisdom and strength and honor and glory and praise!' . . . 'To him who sits on the throne and to the Lamb be praise and honor and glory and power, for ever and ever!'" (Rev. 5:9-13, NIV)."

Worship is an active response to God whereby we declare His worth. Instead of being passive, it is participative. Nor is it simply a mood or feeling, but a declaration of our awe and wonder.

The English word "worship" is wonderfully expressive of the act that it describes. It comes from the Anglo-Saxon *weorthscipe*, which then was modified to "worthship," and finally to worship. Worship means "to attribute worth" to something or someone. When we say of someone that "he worships his money" or that "she worships her children," we are using the word a bit loosely. If, however the supreme worth for him is in his money, or the highest value for her is in her children, then it is an accurate use of the term.

In Great Britain people employ it as the title for the leading citizen of a town: "His Worship the Mayor." In the United States we have changed the phrase to "His Honor the Mayor." To worship someone or something is to attribute supreme worth or to declare supreme value to that individual or thing. If we may elevate this thought to the realm of divine-human relationships, we have a working definition of the term *worship* ready-made for us. To worship God is to ascribe to Him supreme worth, for He alone is worthy.

Because of who God is and what He does, we attribute to Him the glory that is due His name. Such is the strong sentiment of Psalm 96:7, 8:

"Give to the Lord, O families of the peoples,
Give to the Lord glory and strength.
Give to the Lord the glory due His name;
Bring an offering, and come into His courts" (NKJV).

Actually worship is an attitude—an attitude toward God, one that recognizes that He is the Lord, the Creator, and the Savior and King. He is worthy of my adoration, worthy of my submission, worthy of my obedience, worthy of my love, and worthy of my enthusiasm.

Thus worship is our personal response to a divine revelation. We haven't really worshipped until we've responded. Then—and only then—do we want to obey Him, submit to Him, and accept His will.

Worship is not a religious activity that we perform out of duty or observe as a spectator. It is something we need to experience. Instead of something to watch, it is something we become involved in—a giving as well as a receiving event.

Scripture affirms that true worship is the *adoring response to God of sinners saved by grace.* Such adoration may be experienced alone or in a corporate setting. A few biblical examples may suffice to illustrate this view of worship.

Biblical Examples of Worship

ISAIAH'S EXPERIENCE (ISA. 6:1-8)

"In the year that King Uzziah died, I saw the Lord sitting on a throne, high and lifted up, and the train of His robe filled the temple. Above it stood seraphim; each one had six wings: with two he covered his face, with two he covered his feet, and with two he flew. And one cried to another and said: 'Holy, holy, holy is the Lord of hosts; the whole earth is full of His glory!' And the posts of the door were shaken by the voice of him who cried out, and the house was filled with smoke. So I said: 'Woe is me, for I am undone! Because I am a man of unclean lips, and I dwell in the midst of a people of unclean lips; for my eyes have seen the King, the Lord of hosts.' Then one of the seraphim flew to me, having in his hand a live coal which he had taken with the tongs from the altar. And he touched my mouth with it, and said: 'Behold, this has touched your lips; your iniquity is taken away and your sin purged.' Also I heard the voice of the Lord, saying: 'Whom shall I send, and who will go for Us?' Then I said, 'Here am I! Send me'" (NKJV).

WORSHIP IS ABOUT AN ENCOUNTER WITH GOD

We have glanced at this incident in the previous chapter, but let us look at it in even more detail. Isaiah found himself in the ancient Temple after the death of King Uzziah, who had reigned over Judah for 52 years. It was a time of national crisis, when—as the tendency is at such occasions—people flocked to the Temple. As Isaiah worshipped he saw "the Lord sitting up on a throne, high and lifted up" (verse 1). He viewed God as a great king whose robe illuminated the atmosphere. Cherubim and seraphim surrounded Him, symbolizing His eternalness and power. Burning incense, representing God's presence, filled the Temple.

Isaiah's worship began with a clear vision (or revelation) of God—His presence, His majesty, His holiness, and His power. The prophet had a powerful sense of the glory and awesomeness of God that humbled him. The impact of what God is led him to feel the sinfulness of his own nature and to confess, "Woe is me: for . . . I am a man of unclean lips, and I dwell in the midst of a people of unclean lips; for mine eyes have seen the King, the Lord of hosts" (verse 5). His encounter with God made him intensely aware of his own emptiness and helplessness.

Then Isaiah experienced the gospel as he received cleansing, renewal, and empowerment. He saw one of the seraphim, having a burning coal in his hand, fly to him and touch his mouth with the flame, saying, "Your iniquity is taken away" (verse 7, NKJV). The certainty of God's forgiveness gave the prophet a sense of self-worth, devotion, and renewal. God's plea "Whom shall I send, and who will go for us?" (verse 8) touched him. Isaiah suddenly became aware of his own place in God's plan. In surrender he responded, "Here am I! Send me" (verse 8, NKJV). For Isaiah, the worship event determined his future career as he accepted the call to service.

But note again what happened: Isaiah had a *revelation* of God's majesty that overwhelmed him with a sense of personal unworthiness. But he realized that he was forgiven, restored, renewed, and commissioned. These dynamics describe a *relational event* in which God was *"re-seen"* and a human being was *"re-made."* Indeed, it was an event that portrays the adoring response to God of a sinner saved by grace.

21

True worship takes place when we have an encounter with God. When we see Him high and lifted up in all of His holiness and greatness, it will lead us to recognize our emptiness and helplessness. But we are not left there alone. Once we have such an encounter with God, He assures us of His acceptance. The result is love expressed in devotion, commitment, and service.

His encounter with God transformed Isaiah. The same thing happened to Moses. He went to the mountain to see God, and the experience changed him forever. When he came down from the mountain, people were able to tell from the glow on his countenance that he had seen the Lord face to face. God intends that worship will do the same to all of us. When we touch the heart of God, our hearts are warmed, our lives are changed, and people will be able to see in our faces His shining grace and love. Have an encounter with God, and you will never be the same again.

THE SAMARITAN WOMAN (JOHN 4:1-26)

"Therefore, when the Lord knew that the Pharisees had heard that Jesus made and baptized more disciples than John (though Jesus Himself did not baptize, but His disciples), He left Judea and departed again to Galilee. But He needed to go through Samaria.

"So He came to a city of Samaria which is called Sychar, near the plot of ground that Jacob gave to his son Joseph. Now Jacob's well was there. Jesus therefore, being wearied from His journey, sat thus by the well. It was about the sixth hour.

"A woman of Samaria came to draw water. Jesus said to her, 'Give Me a drink.' For His disciples had gone away into the city to buy food.

"Then the woman of Samaria said to Him, 'How is it that You, being a Jew, ask a drink from me, a Samaritan woman?' For Jews have no dealings with Samaritans.

"Jesus answered and said to her, 'If you knew the gift of God, and who it is who says to you, "Give Me a drink," you would have asked Him, and He would have given you living water.'

"The woman said to Him, 'Sir, You have nothing to draw with, and the well is deep. Where then do You get that living water? Are You greater than our father Jacob, who gave us the well, and drank from it himself, as well as his sons and his livestock?'

"Jesus answered and said to her, 'Whoever drinks of this water will thirst again, but whoever drinks of the water that I shall give him will never thirst. But the water that I shall give him will become in him a fountain of water springing up into everlasting life.'

"The woman said to Him, 'Sir, give me this water, that I may not thirst, nor come here to draw.'

"Jesus said to her, 'Go, call your husband, and come here.'

"The woman answered and said, 'I have no husband.'

"Jesus said to her, 'You have well said, "I have no husband," for you have had five husbands, and the one whom you now have is not your husband; in that you spoke truly.'

"The woman said to Him, 'Sir, I perceive that You are a prophet. Our fathers worshiped on this mountain, and you Jews say that in Jerusalem is the place where one ought to worship.'

"Jesus said to her, 'Woman, believe Me, the hour is coming when you will neither on this mountain, nor in Jerusalem, worship the Father. You worship what you do not know; we know what we worship, for salvation is of the Jews. But the hour is coming, and now is, when the true worshipers will worship the Father in spirit and truth; for the Father is seeking such to worship Him. God is Spirit, and those who worship Him must worship in spirit and truth.'

"The woman said to Him, 'I know that Messiah is coming'(who is called Christ). 'When He comes, He will tell us all things.'

"Jesus said to her, 'I who speak to you am He'" (NKJV).

WORSHIP IS ABOUT THE EXPERIENCE OF FORGIVENESS AND RENEWAL OF LIFE

Jesus and His disciples had arrived in Sychar, a small town in Samaria, about a half mile away from Jacob's well. Tired from the journey, He sat down to rest at the well while His disciples went to buy food. When a Samaritan woman arrived to draw water, "Jesus said to her, 'Give me a drink'" (verse 7, NKJV). The woman, recognizing Jesus as a Jew, expressed dismay that a Jew should ask a favor from a Samaritan. She knew very well that the Jews despised Samaritans. But by asking her to do Him a favor, Jesus wanted to make her feel at ease.

Just as her concern about their national differences seemed to be waning, Jesus surprised her the second time. "Go, call your husband, and come here" (verse 16, NKJV). "I have no husband," she admitted (verse 17).

Jesus proceeded to disclose information about her that she could hardly believe a stranger would know. She had just had a *revelation*. "Sir, I perceive that You are a prophet" (verse 19, NKJV). The revelation that she received wasn't only about herself, but about someone who had her interest at heart.

The conversation then shifted to questions about worship and about Gerizim and Jerusalem, traditional places of worship for Samaritans and Jews. But why talk about worship? Because for both Jews and Samaritans, worship meant *sacrifice,* and sacrifice meant *forgiveness, renewal,* and even *salvation.* The Samaritan woman required forgiveness and renewal of life. She actually needed Jesus to renew her so that she could worship Him "in spirit and in truth" (verse 23).

The biblical account then relates that the disciples returned from their errand in the town. Meanwhile the woman left her jar at the well and rushed to her friends with an invitation and testimony: "Come, see a Man who told me all things that I ever did. Could this be the Christ?" (verse 29, NKJV).

The story concludes wonderfully. "And many of the Samaritans of that city believed in Him because of the word of the woman who testified, 'He told me all that I ever did'" (verse 39, NKJV). In short, they all experienced that *adoring response to God of a sinner saved by grace,* and that is what we call worship.

In His conversation with the Samaritan woman Jesus asked and answered two more questions. Where and when do we worship? In Jerusalem, in the church, or does it take place somewhere else? His answer is that worship takes place anywhere, all the time, and under all circumstances. Worship is not bound by place or time or even internal or external factors. It is the experience of a heart that has been in touch with the heart of God and spills over in love, adoration, praise, and devotion.

THE EARLY CHURCH (ACTS 2:42-47)

"And they continued steadfastly in the apostles' doctrine and fellowship, in the breaking of bread, and in prayers. Then fear came upon every soul, and many wonders and signs were done through the apostles. Now all who believed were together, and had all things in common, and sold their possessions and goods, and divided them among all, as anyone had need.

"So continuing daily with one accord in the temple, and breaking bread from house to house, they ate their food with gladness and simplicity of heart, praising God and having favor with all the people. And the Lord added to the church daily those who were being saved" (NKJV).

WORSHIP IS ABOUT A LIFE FULLY DEVOTED TO GOD

In the early church, as recorded in the book of Acts, worship found expression within a unique context (see Acts 2:42). The apostles' teaching, which in turn was founded upon the Old Testament scriptures and the teaching of Christ, *nurtured* the community. Its members' relations with God and one another were bonded in *fellowship,* and were celebrated in *worship.* Such community interaction fulfilled the gospel commission. So the church grew as "the Lord added to the church daily those who were being saved" (verse 47, NKJV).

Worship as exaltation! Let's think about that some more in the context of Acts 2. The church had just been born. Pentecost was the second great feast of the Jewish year, a harvest festival when the people presented the firstfruits of the wheat harvest to God. The resurrection of Jesus, some 50 days earlier, was still the most talked-about event in Jerusalem. The disciples saw what had happened and their response was most appropriate indeed—meeting together, breaking bread, and praising God. Yes, *celebration* was the order of the day.

The focus of Pentecost was clearly God-directed. The crowd who heard the disciples speak in tongues testified that they heard them declaring "the wonderful works of God" (verse 11). True worship is always centered on praise to God because of "his saving acts" throughout history (see Judges 5:11; 1 Sam. 12:7).

Only a few weeks earlier God had revealed Himself in His most supreme "saving act"—Christ's death and resurrection. It was cause for celebration then, and it remains a cause for an adoring, joyous response to God from us today—sinners as we are, saved by His grace.

Give thanks to the Lord, call on his name;

Make known among the nations what he has done.

Sing to him, sing praise to him;

Tell all of his wonderful acts.

Glory in his holy name;

let the hearts of those who seek the Lord rejoice" (Ps. 105: 1-3, NIV).

"Through Jesus, therefore, let us continually offer to God a sacrifice of praise—the fruit of lips that confess his name" (Heb. 13:15, NIV).

3

A Biblical Model of Worship

*I*n the experience of Isaiah, in Jesus' discussion about worship with the woman at Jacob's well, and in the worship of the New Testament church, some distinct dynamics seem to interplay. They are adoration, exaltation, and submission. Each of them appears in some form of expression, and they strengthened the divinely initiated relationship between God and the individual. The same elements characterize a corporate worship event.

No one of them necessarily comes before or after another—for the Holy Spirit works as He pleases. Yet, seldom would one truly worship without sharing the inner precincts of God's presence. Both Old and New Testament Scriptures record the testimonies of those who worshipped God in adoration, exaltation, and submission.

ADORATION

All meaningful worship begins with adoration. God does not need our veneration as much as we need to give it. Adoration is like a channel of communion with God. When we think about His nature, we become open to experience afresh His glory in our lives. I read that in creative conversation there can be no deep exchange with another person until we have established the value of that person to us. Just as profound, conversation with another person results from our communicating to that person his or her worth to us, so too we become receptive to what God wants to do in our lives when we have taken time to tell Him what He means to us.

The difference between adoration and admiration is that adoration always leads to submission. In the strict sense of the word, adoration is an expression by an outward—but even much more by an inward—act of humanity's sincere conviction that its first duty to God is to bow in humility to His power and will.

Tell God what He means to you. Pour out your heart in unhurried moments of adoration. Allow Him to remind you of aspects of His nature that you need to claim. The more we adore the Lord, the more we will be able to think His thoughts, accept His vision, and do His will. He transforms our brains to enable them to become channels of His Spirit.

I've found it helpful to begin my worship experience by first preparing my heart to receive the Holy Spirit. I start by reading the Bible and dwelling on God's work and attributes, letting the Word influence me and change me. Then I start telling God what He means to me. "I love You, Lord. Let me tell You why." Next I rehearse in my mind all that He's been for me. Soon He takes over and leads me in remembering His goodness and grace. During times of difficulty it lifts dark moods, transforms troubled spirits, and makes an unwilling heart receptive. And in bright times of success and smooth sailing, it turns my happiness into pure joy. But whatever the circumstances of life, adoration creates the overwhelming delight of being in the presence of the Lord. Worship, in the ancient sense of the word, means establishing the worth, the wonder, and the glory of God in our minds and hearts. Adoration is the beginning of powerful worship. The Lord created us to receive and return His love.

God wants us to express our love to Him. He longs to hear us say: "Lord, I love You; Lord, I adore You; Lord, I worship You; Lord, I thank

You, because of who You are and because of Your majesty and greatness."

Adoration reminds us who God is and the greatness of His character. It keeps us aware of whose presence we have entered and whose attention we have gained. How often our problems and trials and needs seem so pressing that we reduce worship to self-preoccupation! But when we commit ourselves to adoration, we have to slow down and focus our attention on God Himself.

Often I begin my worship, whether private or corporate, by saying, "Lord, I worship You for being omnipotent." When I say that, I'm reminded that God is able to help me, no matter how difficult my problem seems. I also worship Him for His omniscience. No mystery confounds God. He will not have to scratch His head about anything I say. Thus I worship God for His omnipresence. Wherever I'm praying—in a church, in an airplane, in my car, or in my office—I know He is present with me.

You can adore God for being faithful, righteous, just, merciful, gracious, willing to provide, attentive, and unchanging. When in a spirit of adoration you begin going through God's attributes, you will soon say from the heart, "I am worshipping a marvelous God!"

Adoration also is the means that God uses to purify us. When we have spent a few minutes praising and adoring the Lord for who He is, it softens our spirit and changes our agenda. Those burning issues we were dying to bring to His attention may seem less crucial. Our sense of desperation subsides as we focus on His greatness, and we can truly say, "I am enjoying You, God—it is well with my soul." Above all, adoration purges our spirit and prepares us to listen to Him.

Adoration manifests itself in affirmation of God's goodness. In its essence it is recognizing God's worthiness in everything.

EXALTATION

While reverence and adoration are basically passive responses, exaltation is an active one in which we audibly (or in our thoughts) "lift up" the Lord. *Exalt* means "to raise high; to elevate; to dignify; to magnify; to extol; to glorify; to lift up with joy and pride." When we exalt the Lord, we praise His dignity, His power, and His attributes. We thank Him for what He has done and express our joy at being His children.

"Oh, give thanks to the Lord! Call upon His name; make known His deeds among the peoples! Sing to Him, sing psalms to Him; talk of all His wondrous works! Glory in His holy name; let the hearts of those rejoice who seek the Lord!" (Ps. 105:1-3, NKJV).

The passage is rich with meaning for the worshipper. *Give thanks, make known His deeds, sing psalms, talk of His name, be glad*—all of these are elements of exaltation and commands that the psalms constantly repeat.

The New Testament reiterates the theme. "Let us continually offer the sacrifice of praise to God, that is, the fruit of our lips, giving thanks to His name" (Heb. 13:15, NKJV). Don't just praise Him now and then on special occasions or in carefully created settings. Worship Him always, everywhere. Learn to live with a constant attitude of praise and thanksgiving.

As we have repeatedly emphasized, *worship* means "to attribute worth" to something or someone. For Christians, the object of our worship is God. So true Christian worship is an active response to the Lord whereby we declare His worth. In worship we consciously focus our attention on *who* God is and *what* He has already done and promises to do in the future. Worship is not just a carefully designed ritual, nor is it simply a feeling or a mood or a passive acknowledgment of God's existence and authority. Rather, it is an active, directed, conscious, meaningful exaltation of who He is.

"Though now you do not see Him, yet believing, you rejoice with joy inexpressible and full of glory" (1 Peter 1:8, NKJV).

That is true worship. Not a solemn duty, but a high privilege and matchless delight. "Shout for joy to the Lord. . . . Come before him with joyful songs" (Ps. 100:1, 2, NIV). Such verses paint for us the picture of a celebration of our great and glorious God!

Arturo Toscanini had just finished conducting a brilliant performance of Beethoven's Fifth Symphony. There followed a moment of stunned silence, and then, as though one person, the audience rose to its feet and applauded and shouted its approval. Toscanini waved his arms violently for it all to stop. Pointing to himself, he shouted, "I am nothing!" Then he exclaimed, "Beethoven is everything, everything, everything."

That's the way it is with us and God: we are nothing, and He is everything, everything, everything! In our worship and our work, it is the beginning of wisdom to realize this.

At the heart of exaltation is rejoicing in the cross of Christ. "May I never boast except in the cross of our Lord Jesus Christ, through which the world has been crucified to me, and I to the world" (Gal. 6:14, NIV).

Exaltation always manifests itself in praise and thanksgiving.

"Give thanks to the Lord, call on his name; make known among the nations what he has done. Sing to him, sing praise to him; tell of all his wonderful acts. Glory in his holy name; let the hearts of those who seek the Lord rejoice" (1 Chron. 16:8-10, NIV).

"Shout for joy to the Lord, all the earth. Worship the Lord with gladness; come before him with joyful songs. Know that the Lord is God. It is he, who made us, and we are his; we are his people, the sheep of his pasture" (Ps. 100:1-3, NIV).

Exaltation usually leads to giving the Lord everything we have.

"Bring an offering and come before him; worship the Lord in the splendor of his holiness" (1 Chron. 16:29, NIV).

"Each man should give what he has decided in his heart to give, not reluctantly or under compulsion, for God loves a cheerful giver" (2 Cor. 9:7, NIV).

"'Bring the whole tithe into the storehouse, that there may be food in my house. Test me in this,' says the Lord Almighty, 'and see if I will not throw open the floodgates of heaven and pour out so much blessing that you will not have room enough for it'" (Mal. 3:10, NIV).

SUBMISSION

Our worship of God begins with adoration and exaltation, but it doesn't end there. As we have already noted, the natural outgrowth of worship and adoration is submission. When I quiet myself before God and concentrate on *who* He is and *what* He has done for me, I can do nothing but submit to Him. If I have really caught a glimpse of His majesty, His power, His mercy, His loving-kindness, and all else that He is, I will be irresistibly drawn to commit myself to pleasing and obeying Him.

The Greek and Hebrew words for "worship" (*proskyneo* and the Hebrew equivalent *shachah*) had the meaning "to be brought low," "to humble oneself," "to have one's arrogance knocked out of him," and "to serve the Lord in complete submission" (see Isa. 2:11, 17; Ps. 107:39; Job 9:13).

When Satan tempted Jesus by promising the kingdoms of this world if He would fall down and worship the devil, the Lord rebuked him: "For it is written, 'You shall *worship* [*proskyneo*] the Lord your God, and Him only you shall serve'" (Matt. 4:10, NKJV). Both the Old Testament and the New Testament express humanity's relationship to God in terms of service and obedience. Human beings are God's servants or slaves. They demonstrate their worship of God in terms of faithfulness, service, and obedience.

In Gethsemane Jesus said, "Not My will, but Yours, be done" (Luke 22:42, NKJV). Like Him, we too must give voice to our willingness to cast off our own personal aspirations and selfish desires and consciously submit ourselves to His designs.

"Therefore humble yourselves under the mighty hand of God" (1 Peter 5:6, NKJV). That is what we do in worship. First we stand silent before God in reverence. Then we bow down before Him in submission. We acknowledge and welcome His authority, and commit ourselves to faithful obedience. If we worship Him from any other position, we present Him with nothing more than an empty ritual.

Too often when we think of worship we regard it as going to church to hear a sermon. Now, you may listen to 10 powerful, polished, elegant, original sermons, and still you have not worshipped if you have not responded and made a commitment to live out the demands of Jesus. Yet you could be a worshipper if after hearing just two verses you make a decision to live your faith. Worship is experienced only when you give worth to God—honor Him with glory, adoration, and praise.

But all too often we settle for flabby worship. The vast majority of Christians—even born-again believers—are pew fillers, hymn singers, sermon tasters, but not true worshippers of Jesus. If we were willing to become true worshippers it would transform the church, and the impact on society would be staggering. This is no idle claim—it happened in the first century. The Christian church is not a club that we belong to so that it will meet our needs. Rather, it is a family that exists to worship God and give Him glory, honor, and majesty.

Abraham demonstrated his worship to God in the act of communion with God. His experience demonstrated that worship is not one-way communion. God and Abraham engaged in a love relationship. Worship, in this sense, is authentic communion, a genuine fellowship with God. Close communion and intimate fellowship make possible deep and lasting worship.

The deep adoration and awe that compelled Abraham to fall on his face and worship God (Gen. 17:3) repudiates any suggestion of flippancy and carelessness. When one fails to sense the glory and majesty of the Creator God, faith can easily turn into presumption and worship into self-glorification.

So, again, what is worship? It is adoration, exaltation, and submission. Through adoration we acknowledge God's worth. Submission testifies that we recognize and accept His authority. And through exaltation we lift Him up with our expressions of adoration. That, in summary, is *true* worship.

A PERSONAL RESPONSE

My daughter, who is away at college in Keene, Texas, called yesterday and said, "Dad, I can hardy wait to be with you next weekend. I love you so much!"

It was just one short sentence, but what joy and excitement those words brought me! I will never tire of overhearing those spontaneous praises, of feeling loving arms encircling my neck, accompanied by an un-solicited "I love you, Daddy." Why? Because I *love* my children! In fact, I love them so much that what they think of me is just about the most important thing in the world. I receive a tremendous amount of pleasure from knowing that they love me and appreciate the things that I do for them. My deep love for them makes their responses very important.

Isn't it the same with God? Though I do not claim to understand completely why God desires our worship, I'm certain that part of His reason is the pure joy of hearing our heartfelt reaction to His unfathomable love. Having created and redeemed us, He has called us by name and loved us with an everlasting love.

Shouldn't we expect Him to desire our loving response?

When I was in Nigeria teaching some classes at Babcock University, I had plenty of time to think about my wife, Denise, and remember the special things that she had done for me and to appreciate her role in my life. Often my thoughts led to such feelings of love that I just had to call and tell her how I felt. Since I did not have a telephone in my room, I had to use a university phone. Though that arrangement was far from convenient and very expensive, the calls were well worth the effort and the cost.

So it is with worship. As love and not duty prompted my telephone calls to Denise, so our offerings of worship should be a means of express-ing not just our resigned obedience, but our sincere love and admiration for our gracious Father.

"Shout for joy to the Lord, all the earth.
Worship the Lord with gladness;
Come before him with joyful songs.
Know that the Lord is God.
It is he who made us, and we are his;
We are his people, the sheep of his pasture.
Enter his gates with thanksgiving
And his courts with praise;
Give thanks to him and praise his name.
For the Lord is good and his love endures forever;
His faithfulness continues through all generations.

4

How to Behave
in a Worshipful Way

Jeff Smith slept in on Sabbath morning. His mom woke him up and said, "You need to get ready to go to church."

"I am not going to church anymore," he announced.

"But you need to go."

"Why? Give me one good reason I should go to church." Then he looked his mother straight in the eye and said, "I find it to be boring, predictable, and irrelevant. No one there loves me or cares about me. It does not meet my needs. Just give me one good reason I should go."

"I will give you two reasons. First of all, you are 30 years old, and you need God. Second, people in church expect you to be there—after all, you are the pastor."

Have you ever felt like Jeff Smith as you attend a church worship service? Why is church so boring sometimes?

I believe that church often bores because it has become a spectator sport—we go to see and hear a program rather than to be engaged and participate.

God intends that our worship should be enthusiastic and participatory and arise out of a life that has been in touch with Him all week.

THE HOW AND WHY OF WORSHIP

Our behavior must be appropriate to the occasion. You don't wear a tuxedo to a ball game. Neither do you wear shorts to your own wedding.

When you come to meet together to worship God, you face the issue of how you behave when you gather as God's people to worship? What's the right attitude?

We gain insight from an ancient hymn that was part of Israel's songbook and that appears in our Bible. Even though it's short, Psalm 100 is full of insights as to how you and I are supposed to conduct ourselves when we worship the Lord.

It is a praise psalm. Praise psalms tend to alternate between giving us instruction on how to worship—the call to praise—and revealing the cause or the reason. That's what happens here. Verses 1 and 2 give us the how, and verse 3 says, "Here's why." Verse 4 makes another call to worship, and tells you how to do it. Then verse 5 offers us the why.

Psalm 100 declares: "Shout for joy to the Lord, all the earth. Worship the Lord with gladness; come before him with joyful songs. Know that the Lord is God. It is he who made us, and we are his; we are his people, the sheep of his pasture. Enter his gates with thanksgiving and his courts with praise; give thanks to him and praise his name. For the Lord is good and his love endures forever; his faithfulness continues through all generations" (NIV).

WORSHIP THE LORD WITH ENTHUSIASM

How do you behave when you come together to worship? Verse 4 mentions entering His gates and His courts. The picture here is of an Old Testament Israelite, a worshipper, coming through the Temple gates and into the courts in which the people had assembled to worship. The psalm speaks of people gathering together and offers instruction on how they ought to worship.

What are we supposed to do when we assemble to worship God? Verse 1 says: "Shout for joy." It is an interesting command, because ancient Israel used it as a battle cry. Joshua 6 tells how Israel marched around the city of Jericho. Verse 16 tells us that the people were supposed to shout—the same word employed here. It's a battle cry. So when people get together to worship God, there ought to be some shouting for victory.

We must have a heart so full of the things of God that they spill over in praise and adoration and thanksgiving. What we need is not a tongue to praise the Lord, although that is helpful. Rather, what we require is a heart fully engaged with the heart of God.

Verse 2 urges us to "worship the Lord with gladness; come before him with joyful songs." Literally, it's a cry or song of joy. You start to get the picture that when God's people assemble to worship God, there ought to be enthusiasm and excitement.

Some of you may be thinking, *But I was taught that we were supposed to be quiet for worship—that if we're going to be reverent, we need to be silent.*

A choir anthem says, "The Lord is in his holy temple; let all the earth be silent before him" (NIV). The concept comes out of Habakkuk 2:20. I got the surprise of my life when I began reading Habakkuk 2 and realized that God was not speaking to worshippers. He was talking to an enemy nation, a group of people who were about to receive divine judgment. The Lord said, "I want you to be quiet, because I am about to exact punishment upon you."

Certainly, you think, the psalms must contain some statements about silence that will help guide us in our worship. Once when I went through the book of Psalms and looked at every reference that mentioned silence I got another surprise. Actually, I received the shock of my life. Most of the time when Psalms talks about silence, it is in the context of judgment and death.

Consider Psalm 115:17: "It is not the dead who praise the Lord, those who go down to silence; it is we who extol the Lord, both now and forevermore" (NIV). References to silence consistently appear in relationship not to worship but rather to judgment and death. Silence, therefore, is something negative. Psalm 31:17 declares, "Let the wicked be put to shame and lie silent in the grave" (NIV).

Does that mean that silence is inappropriate in our worship? No, there are times we need to pause to listen or to reflect on what we've read and what we've learned. The goal is that once we're done with that, we can cut loose in exuberance and in enthusiasm.

We often tell our kids to be quiet. Too often it's the one thing that they learn from attending church. When they finally get it, they begin coming to church saying and doing nothing.

On the other hand, you cannot tell me that being silent is an indication of worship. Every Sabbath morning we find many who are very, very quiet during the worship service (at least some are). They are sound asleep. At least on the surface, very little worship, if any, goes on.

In fact, I read in *Leadership Journal* that in Toronto a man had a heart attack in church and passed out. When the paramedics came, they had to go through three rows of somnolent people before they found the right individual. Being silent in church is not an indication of a worshipful experience.

In one of the churches I pastored I had many young people in my congregation who were into many athletic activities. Many Sundays they went to Seattle to watch the Mariners play. So one Sunday I decided to go with them. Probably 40,000-50,000 people jammed the stadium. Ken Griffey, Jr., who was with the Mariners at that time, hit a home run. The place went crazy. People jumped up and down, giving high fives and shouting. It was a ringing shout, because their man had hit a home run.

The crowd yelled at the top of their lungs, including the 40-50 from my church. That lasted for about five or six minutes. Finally, when they calmed down and took their seats, I stood up and told my group, "Shame on you. Shame on you. You come over here and get excited. You're exuberant. You're cheering and yelling and animated about nothing, but when you attend church you slip into a coma."

Somehow we get the impression that's worship—being silent. Silence may be appropriate in some situations, but if you want to be biblical, the psalms call us to enthusiasm, excitement, and exuberance when we gather to worship.

I'm not saying that you need to give each other high fives or do cartwheels down the aisle, but worship is a time of anticipation and expectation. We assemble together because all week long God has been knocking home runs and scoring touchdowns in our lives. Worship is a time to celebrate what God has done for us. God's counsel to His last-day church is to be more enthusiastic.

"I know your deeds, that you are neither cold nor hot. I wish you were either one or the other! So, because you are lukewarm—neither hot nor cold—I am about to spit you out of my mouth! You say, 'I am rich; I have acquired wealth and do not need a thing.' But you do not realize that you are wretched, pitiful, poor, blind and naked. I counsel you to buy from me gold refined in the fire, so you can become rich; and white clothes to wear, so you can cover your shameful nakedness; and salve to put on your eyes, so you can see. Those whom I love I rebuke and discipline. So be earnest and repent" (Rev. 3:15-19, NIV).

In essence, the message to the Laodicean church commands us to get a life and a heart. "Get out of your lukewarm stage," God declares. "I am sick of your apathetic and lethargic attitude."

So what is reverence? Scripture closely associates it with awe and wonder. Hebrews 12:28 states: "Therefore, since we are receiving a kingdom that cannot be shaken, let us be thankful, and so worship God acceptably with reverence and awe" (NIV). When we stand in front of God and have a vision of His grace, love, majesty, awesomeness, greatness—we say, "Wow! Wow! What a God we worship." Our overpowering sense of wonder will compel us to bow down, casting away our pride and self-interest, and worship the Lord in service and commitment.

The psalmist says that we should not only pass through His gates with thanksgiving, but enter His courts with praise. When you're excited about a person or product, you will proclaim that fact.

The Bible declares that when we come to worship, we ought to boast in our excitement. The God we serve is worthy of our praise, our excitement, and our enthusiasm. The songs we sing, the testimonies we give, often provide us an opportunity to do that.

Then, in case we've missed it, the psalm says: "Give thanks to him and praise his name" (Ps. 100:4, NIV).

Margaret Sangster Phippen wrote that in the mid-1950s her father, British minister W. E. Sangster, began to notice some uneasiness in his throat and a dragging in his leg. When he went to the doctor, he found that he had an incurable disease that caused progressive muscular atrophy.

His muscles would gradually waste away, his voice would fail, and his throat would soon become unable to swallow.

Sangster threw himself into his work in British home missions, figuring that he could still write and that he would have even more time for prayer. "Let me stay in the struggle, Lord," he pleaded. "I don't mind if I can no longer be a general—give me just a regiment to lead." He wrote articles and books and helped organize prayer cells throughout England. "I'm only in the kindergarten of suffering," he told people who pitied him.

Gradually Sangster's legs became useless. His voice went completely silent. But he could still hold a pen, if shakily. On Easter morning, just a few weeks before he died, he wrote a letter to his daughter. "It is terrible to wake up on Easter morning and have no voice to shout, 'He is risen!'" he said in it. "But it would be still more terrible to have a voice and not want to shout."

WORSHIP THE LORD WITH TRUE THANKSGIVING

Yes, we make a joyful noise, but what kind of noise? What's the content of that? Psalm 100:4 tells us to "enter his gates with thanksgiving and his courts with praise; give thanks to him and praise his name" (NIV).

You attend a church picnic, and a woman named Martha has made a wonderful peach pie that melts in your mouth. Afterward you go to her and say, "Martha, thank you for that wonderful peach pie." You know what? You have at that time extended thanks, but in essence you have not yet offered biblical thanksgiving. The word "thanksgiving" means to give public acknowledgment. Until in a group of people you say in her presence, "I want to tell you what a wonderful peach pie Martha made; it melts in your mouth, and it's great," you have not fulfilled this command. That's how it works with God. Biblical thanksgiving is giving public recognition of God's goodness.

Let's suppose that you have sent out dozens of résumés and have had hours of job interviews, and finally you land that perfect job. As you look at the circumstances, you know it was God's hand that was part of it. So in your private prayer time you say, "God, I want to thank You for providing that job." That's great. But you still haven't followed the biblical command. You haven't fulfilled it until in the presence of God's people you stand up and say, "I want to tell you what God has done for me. I finally got the job I needed. It's going to provide for the family. God is the one who made it possible." At that point you have accomplished biblical thanksgiving: public acknowledgment—a sharing with others what God had done.

John says of God's people in Revelation 12:11 that "they overcame . . . by the blood of the Lamb and by the word of their testimony" (NIV).

Do you have anything for which to be thankful? Think of what He has done for you, in you, with you, and promised to you. I truly believe that if we would approach worship with that sort of attitude, our individual worship would improve dramatically. The song "Give Thanks" begins, "Give thanks with a grateful heart." At first that might seems a little redundant. The implication is that we ought to be thankful that within our very hearts we can express our gratitude to God. When we come to church, there ought to be an aura about our worship because of our thankful hearts.

Worship the Lord With Joy

Psalm 100:1 declares that joy should be a significant part of how we worship. I did an extensive study to discover the message of the verse. But it does not really take any great skill to figure out what this verse means. It simply commands us to worship the Lord with gladness. You do not need to discuss it, argue about it, or figure out what the Hebrew means.

When we worship God, there ought to be a certain bounce to ourselves. It should not be forced or artificial, but should flow out of what fills our lives. His joy ought to be ours. We ought to worship the Lord out of the overflow of a life that has His person in it. And when God is your center, your heart will not be able to help spilling over with joy and enthusiasm, because we are His.

The television program *Dateline* broadcast an exposé on the happiness industry—people who go around and for a fee (of course) will help you to be happy. Barry Colfman left his advertising company and started the Option Institute. He said to Maria Shriver, "I want to be your happiness coach. I can teach people how to be happy. They just have to make a decision not to take all the trash the world gives them, and they have to decide to be happy."

Her response to him was "Wouldn't it be wonderful if it were that easy?"

We don't manufacture our happiness. Rather, we are the people with joy that is God-given.

The only reason I am not a candidate for depression or suicide is that God's joy/person/character are in me. It gives me a reason for life. I worship with gladness because I am His. Happiness is available for a price in the U.S. through this medium and that medium. But you cannot buy it— you can't go to a conference and get it. The ability to worship the Lord with gladness has everything to do with us coming to know the Lord and being filled with His Spirit.

The grandparents of our children were in the habit of showering them with love and gifts. When Christmas arrives, and mom and dad say to the children, "Let's go and see grandma and grandpa," will their attitude be "Oh *no,* we have to see our grandma and grandpa"? Or, rather, "We hardly can wait to be there!"?

It is not drudgery for us to be in God's presence. Bathed in the sunshine of His presence, it ought to be our delight to gaze into our heavenly Father's face and enjoy His presence. He is a God who valued our lives on a level with that of His own Son. When we gather on Sabbath or for any religious assembly, we ought to come with a certain gladness and joy because God is God.

The psalmist declares that it ought to be our delight to approach God and enjoy His presence. It presupposes a relationship that makes you want to be there. He says that when we come together to worship God, we ought to rehearse His goodness with joy and gladness. If you have been dragging your feet at being at worship, get over it.

Someone has defined joy as "having inner confidence, knowing that God is in control." It means that God is in charge of every circumstance of our lives. The problems that surround us may seem insurmountable, and we want others to be as miserable as we are. But joy says that "I believe that God is in control of the problems troubling my life right now, and I believe that He is going to work everything out to His glory and honor." Does that mean, however, that we come to worship in a giddy sort of way? We must not confuse happiness and joy. At times sadness is going to be present in our lives, and that is all right. But you will never be happy until there is joy in your heart. You could almost say that our worship is an out-pouring of that joy. To put it in a different way, happiness is the by-product of some happening, while joy is the by-product of the Holy Spirit dwelling in us. But when the Holy Spirit controls our lives, He will produce this kind of fruit in us. Paul states that "the fruit of the Spirit is love, joy, peace, patience, kindness, goodness, faithfulness, gentleness and self-control. Against such things there is no law" (Gal. 5:22, 23, NIV).

Nehemiah declares that the joy of the Lord serves as our strength (Neh. 8:10). When we worship our heavenly Father and His Son, Jesus Christ, there ought to be much joy in our heart. Oftentimes, during the worship hour we look as if we have swallowed some really bad-tasting medicine. You know the expression your children get when they have to take medicine and they curl their nose and twist their lips and act as if they are just about to die. That is often how we come to worship God. While we will always have problems in our lives, we need to have the right perspective about them—that God is in control. We need to look and act as if we truly desire to worship Him.

Paul tells us that one of the fruits of the Spirit is joy. Joy does not depend on what happens to us, how we do in the world, or on the opinion of others. Rather, joy comes to us when God enters our hearts and dwells in us.

We Worship the Lord Because the Lord Is God

We all have days that we don't feel like giving the Lord that kind of enthusiasm, thanksgiving, or joy. If you don't feel like worshipping, then what will revive the desire? Let's go back to the "why" section of Psalm 100.

Verse 3 tells us to "know that the Lord is God." The word Lord is in all capital letters in many English translations. Whenever that shows up in the Old Testament, it indicates the personal name for God—Yahweh. The psalmist thus tells us that Yahweh God made us, and we are His people—the sheep of His pasture whom He cares for. The one who created us, He knows everything about us. That's a reason to be excited about God.

It seems to me that there are two basic questions in relation to the worship of a holy God. First, we have the issue of the manner of worship. That is a question of appropriate form, and will answer the question of how to worship God. But I think there is something even more basic. We wonder why we should worship at all. Now, we might give a number of spiritual responses. But they really do not answer the why question. I have even heard people declare that "it is our duty to worship." But I believe that if you come to worship out of a sense of duty, then you have missed the point.

I hope to answer these two questions through a study of Psalm 95.

We worship the Lord because He is "*the Rock of our salvation*" (verse 1,

NKJV). That Rock is Jesus. First Corinthians 10:4 says of ancient Israel that "they drank of that spiritual Rock that followed them, and that Rock was Christ" (NKJV). Worship is first and foremost about Jesus.

WE WORSHIP THE LORD BECAUSE HE IS OUR SALVATION

We must always keep in mind that, while indeed we accept Him personally as Lord and Savior, it is God who gives us salvation (Ps. 95:1). So I don't pray, "God, I thank You for my salvation." Rather, I pray, "God, thank You for the salvation that You have given to me." A subtle difference exists between the two prayers. The first almost indicates that salvation belongs to me and always has. The second prayer gives the credit to the One who has provided the salvation. When I worship, I come in an attitude of awe, because of God giving salvation to someone as unworthy as I am; to someone as unlovely as I am; to someone as guilty of sin as I am.

WE WORSHIP THE LORD BECAUSE HE IS GREAT!

"The Lord is the great God, and the great King" (verse 3, NKJV). The nations surrounding Israel believed that the Hebrew God was just a local deity—a small God of an insignificant nation, and therefore one of the inferior gods. The psalmist declares that is not the case. Because He is all in all, He is a great king above all other powers and dignitaries. That is why we spell His name with a capital letter. He is not "a" god—He is "the" God.

WE WORSHIP THE LORD BECAUSE HE IS STRONG!

"In His hand are the deep places of the earth; the heights of the hills are His also" (verse 4, NKJV). Not only is He God of the mountains, the valleys, the seas, and the earth, He is God of everything. Psalm 139:7, 8 asks, "Where can I go from Your Spirit? Or where can I flee from Your presence? If I ascend into heaven, You are there; if I make my bed in hell, behold, You are there" (NKJV).

First Corinthians 10:26 tells us that "the earth is the Lord's, and all its fullness" (NKJV). Psalm 8:1, 2 declares: "O Lord, our Lord, how excellent is Your name in all the earth, who have set Your glory above the heavens! Out of the mouth of babes and nursing infants You have ordained strength, because of Your enemies, that You may silence the enemy and the avenger" (NKJV).

We Worship the Lord Because He Is Holy!

"Oh come, let us worship . . .; let us kneel before the Lord our Maker" (Ps. 95:6, NKJV). Ours is a holy privilege to bow before a holy God and worship Him. We are not only believers but worshipers. The spirit of humble adoration is our best fitness for service. It is on bowed knees and with humble hearts that one gains victory in life. Jeremiah 10:6 reminds us: "Inasmuch as there is none like You, O Lord (You are great, and Your name is great in might)" (NKJV).

We Worship the Lord Because He Is Gracious!

"We are the people of His pasture, and the sheep of His hand" (Ps. 95:7, NKJV). Daily He feeds and protects us. Our pastures are not ours, but His—we draw all our supplies from His stores. Charles Spurgeon once said, "We are His, even as sheep belong to the shepherd, and His hand is our rule, our guidance, our government, our succor, our source of supply."

We Worship the Lord Because He Is Good

Why should we worship the Lord? Psalm 100:5 says, "For the Lord is good" (NIV).

I wish it were more "meaty" for you. But it all boils down to one fundamental fact: you worship the Lord with joyful song and praise of thanksgiving because the Lord is good—because He has lavished His goodness on you.

When we meet to worship Sabbath after Sabbath, day after day, or however often you do it, we are in essence rehearsing the goodness of God. The Lord has brought us together another time, given us one more opportunity to live. Because He has been good to us, we worship Him.

The phrase "For the Lord is good" has become one of the most vital parts of this psalm for me. Maybe that's because, as a pastor, I often have to deal with sin's fallout and pain. I encounter people every week who have had a lot of bad experiences at the hands of those who should have been good to them. Sometimes it breaks my heart when such individuals leave my office.

I've shed tears with people who have told me stories about how as children they have suffered evil at the hands of a parent or a loved one. I am so thankful that the God I serve is not like that—He is a God who is good, whom I can trust, and who's never going to hurt me. Such is the kind of God we serve, and I can get excited about that.

WE WORSHIP THE LORD BECAUSE HIS LOVING-KINDNESS ENDURES FOREVER

Verse 5 goes on to add: "And his love endures forever" (NIV). That word "love "could be the most important word in the Old Testament. Some modern translations render it as "lovingkindness." Others employ "mercy." I like to translate the Hebrew word as "loyal love," because it is a two-pronged word. On the one hand, it describes affection—God has affection and passion for us as His people. The other side is a covenant word. Some people translate it as "covenant love." It has a commitment aspect to it—staying power. Not only does God have feeling for us, but He has a commitment that He will not break.

To put it simply, God is madly in love with you.

God is crazy about you.

God is committed to you.

To help you grasp more of the significance of the Hebrew word we have been talking about, let me tell you something about the ancient Israelites. They were bird watchers even though they didn't have eight-power binoculars and a tattered copy of *Birds of Southern Palestine*. But as they watched birds they observed some things that they liked and some they didn't.

One of the birds they did not like was the ostrich. The ostrich would lay its eggs anywhere, even in the middle of a pathway. The bird was fast, but that was part of the problem. As soon as trouble came, the creature would race away. Such behavior disturbed the Israelites.

But the stork they did admire, because when it laid its eggs it put them in a nest on top of a tree or in the crags of a cliff. Then the stork would stay with its eggs. Even if a predator threatened it, the stork stuck it out.

The Hebrews took the word that I have translated as "loyal love" (*hesed*), changed a couple of letters, and used it to form a name of that bird. They called the stork a *hasidah*, because they were so enthralled with the creature's staying power. *Hesed* indicates that God has affection for us, but He also has a commitment that will never let us go. God is willing to put His life on the line for us because He loves us.

I can get excited about worshipping a God like that.

A friend of mine from college, Glen, became interested in a young woman, Tara, who was part of the group that we hung out with. One day he got the courage to ask her out. She said no. A week later he tried again. Again she told him no. Two weeks later he tried one more time. And one more time she answered no. So he changed his strategy by starting to do all kinds of wonderful things for her. He sent her flowers one week and chocolates another week and yet another week he gave her cookies and candy. Finally she said, "Yes, but with a group." After a few weeks the group just disappeared, and the two of them went on a date together. Two years later, when he asked her to marry him, she said yes.

That was 25 years ago. Today they are living a happy and content life.

My friend's love for Tara was so compelling, so strong, and so focused that he kept pursuing her. He would not let her go. God's love is like that. His love will follow you no matter what—no matter what you do, where you come from, where you go. Divine love will be after you whether you are tall or short, ugly or beautiful, smart or dumb, likable or not—whether you love Him or hate Him. It does not matter to God. He is madly in love with you. Nothing you can do will remove you from His love. I want to worship a God like that.

We Worship the Lord Because His Faithfulness Endures Forever

Finally, in verse 5, we learn that His faithfulness continues through all generations, a concept that appears in Ruth 4:16. In describing Naomi and the grandson born to her daughter-in-law, Ruth, it declares that Naomi became faithful to that baby.

Scripture uses that same word for the pillars in the Temple. It portrays a picture of security and support—that those pillars would hold up that structure no matter what happened. The Bible writers employed the same word to present a similar picture of God: when we get in tough situations and even when we are unfaithful, God is still there to support us.

Many bad things most likely happened to the Temple—rain, earthquake, lightning, snow, windstorms—but because the pillars were so strong, it was able to withstand them. In the same way, many bad things strike us, leading to pain, unemployment, illness, death; but we can remember that God is always there for us.

A PERSONAL APPEAL

When you arrive at church Sabbath morning and don't feel like worshipping, what should you do? Don't try to force yourself—that doesn't work. When I get to church and don't feel in a worshipful mood—and there are days like that—I do not try to manufacture my emotion so that it will appear that I'm doing what I'm supposed to. No, the best thing I've found is to reflect on the character of God.

Do you see why worship should be so enthusiastic? why God tells us not to be silent but to shout for joy? Worship should be a response to the awesomeness of the God that we serve.

As a young boy I used to get bored with church. My mom would tell me to pray that God would prepare my heart for worship by helping me see His greatness. The more we recognize that, the more we will be inclined to worship.

We can get in the mode for worship in two different ways.

The first thing we need to do is to prepare our hearts for it by reading the Bible, especially the Psalms, and reminding ourselves of God's character and attributes. He is holy, just, loving, gracious, powerful, merciful—the great I AM, the door, the way, the truth, the life, the one that sticks closer than a brother, the Lord, the Savior. The more we know about God, the more we will want to worship Him.

Second, we must cultivate a tremendous hunger and desire to have an encounter with the Lord. That hunger comes from constantly increasing our knowledge of God and from asking Him to give us this desire. When you have that encounter with Him, your life will change, your dreams will be aligned with His, and your face will reflect His glory and love.

The hand that separated the waters at the Red Sea and brought forth water out of the rock is still with us, working equal wonders. Can we refuse to worship and bow down when we clearly see that this God is our God for ever and ever, and will be our guide even to death?

God grant that you worship Him with gladness and not drudgery.

God grant that you worship Him with praise and thanksgiving, because His love is always and forever.

*"Rejoice always, pray without ceasing, in everything give thanks;
for this is the will of God in Christ Jesus for you"*

(1 Thess. 5:16-18, NKJV).

*"Be anxious for nothing, but in everything by prayer and supplication,
with thanksgiving, let your requests be made known to God"*

(Phil. 4:6, NKJV).

5

Prayer and Worship

How do you view prayer in general? What do you consider its purpose? Is it simply to draw up a list of requests and petitions and problems and present them in an acceptable fashion to God? Or is it to become aware of God's answers and guidance? He doesn't instruct us to pray without ceasing just so that He can be the genie that fulfills all of our wants and needs.

The purpose of prayer goes deeper than that. Prayer is a way to maintain constant and meaningful communion with God. It is about knowing Him, worshipping Him, loving Him, adoring Him, and having a deep, passionate, and intense relationship with Him. Through prayer we become aware of God's presence, His activities, His grace—aware of everything that has to do with our heavenly Father.

Prayer glorifies God by demonstrating the utter dependency that His children show toward Him. Through it we experience divine forgiveness, power, wisdom, joy, love, compassion, and confidence.

Let's look more closely at prayer and its role in worship.

PRAYER IS SEEKING GOD'S PRESENCE

God has always a hunger and desire to be with us. Creation is about God being with us. The sanctuary is about God being with us. Jesus is Immanuel, which means "God with us." When Jesus went to heaven, He sent the Holy Spirit to be with us. The Second Coming is about the ultimate presence of God with His people. The most fundamental want and desire that He has is to be with us.

The Old Testament tells of many ways that He let His people know that He was among them: through the tabernacle that accompanied Israel on its journeys; through His Shekinah glory that rested over the ark in the Temple; and through a whole succession of prophets that spoke His Word to the people.

Going to the Bible, I discovered that throughout recorded history God has taken pains to emphasize how He dwelled among His people. After leading the Israelites out of Egypt and into the desert on their way to the Promised Land, God knew they would feel frightened and alone. They camped in a place with wild animals, little food, and practically no water. Israel had no armies and no walls to protect them from enemy attack.

In their heads they knew that they were God's people and that He had promised to defend them. But it was hard to feel His presence. And so the Lord, seeking to convince them that He was with them wherever they went, gave them a visible sign of His presence. "And the Lord went before them by day in a pillar of cloud to lead the way, and by night in a pillar of fire to give them light, so as to go by day and night" (Ex. 13:21, NKJV). If ever the people began to wonder if their journey was headed in the right direction, all they had to do was look up and see the pillar of cloud. Or if they grew frightened of animals, or of enemies that might be stalking them, they could glance at the pillar of fire casting its glow over the whole camp. God made sure that they could feel His presence in their midst.

The New Testament begins with God offering us His presence in the person of Jesus Christ, His Son. The promised Baby was to be called

Immanuel, "God with us" (Matt. 1:23). John explains the significance of Jesus' birth: "And the Word became flesh and dwelt among us" (John 1:14, NKJV). Theologians call this the *Incarnation*—God putting on human flesh and actually living with His people.

His presence through Jesus was powerful. It transformed ordinary, sinful people into apostles who "turned the world upside down" (Acts 17:6, NKJV). Even unbelieving leaders recognized what it was that made the difference in such individuals: "When they saw the courage of Peter and John and realized that they were unschooled, ordinary men, they were astonished and they took note that these men had been with Jesus" (Acts 4:13, NIV).

But, as powerful as God's presence in Christ was, it still lacked something. Jesus' ministry on earth lasted only about three and a half years. He never left Palestine. Only a relatively small number of people ever met Him personally. The vast majority of those who have lived on earth have never come in direct contact with Him. That is why Jesus promised His disciples, "I will ask the Father, and he will give you another Counselor to be with you forever—the Spirit of truth" (John 14:16, 17, NIV).

Shortly after Jesus ascended to the Father, that promise was fulfilled. On the day of Pentecost God sent the Holy Spirit to take up permanent residence in the lives of His followers.

Ever since then, all believers have a strong sign of God's presence with them. The moment you bow to Christ and become His, God cleanses you of your sin and simultaneously fills you with His Holy Spirit. As time passes you grow to realize you are never alone. God's presence is real. You can feel it. It's with you wherever you go.

When you practice being aware of God's presence, you pick up His signals all through the day. At work, at home, in your car, or wherever you are, you begin to dialog with the Lord. You share your heart with Him, and you know that He's listening. It has nothing to do with being in a church building or on your knees but with the divine presence in and around you—"Christ in you, the hope of glory" (Col. 1:27, NIV).

Brother Lawrence, a cook in a seventeenth-century French monastery, gave the world a phrase that well describes such a deep friendship with Jesus: *the practice of the presence of God.* As the humble monk cleaned stairs and bedrooms, washed dishes, and served food to his fellow monastics, he communed with God, and the glow of His presence gave Lawrence's menial kitchen duties richness and significance. I have been a Christian all my life, but only recently have I started to practice God's presence in my own life. From Brother Lawrence I learned that in my car, on the job, at home, while working out, while helping somebody move, while lying in bed at night—anytime, anywhere, under any circumstances, I could commune meaningfully with the Lord. God is near me and wants to enjoy a friendship with me.

If Jesus were to talk to me personally, He would say, "I want to relate to you as your forgiver and Lord, but I also want to be your best friend. I want our conversations to bring you comfort, peace, and joy. I want to shadow you all day long. And I'd like for you to think about Me all day long. I want you to know that you're never alone. Wherever you go and whatever you do, I will be at your side. I want you to discover My presence in your daily life. I am going to be your companion." That is what we mean when we say that prayer is being aware of God's presence.

PRAYER IS SEEKING GOD'S GLORY

Hear Jesus' words in John 14:13: "Whatever you ask in My name, that will I do, so that the Father may be glorified in the Son" (NASB). Suppose that you are totally paralyzed and can do nothing for yourself but talk. And suppose a strong and reliable friend promised to live with you and do whatever you needed done. How would you praise your friend if a stranger came to see you? Would you glorify that friend's generosity and strength by trying to get out of bed and carrying him or her? No! You would say, "Friend, please come lift me up, and would you put a pillow behind me so that I can look at my guest?" As a result your visitor would learn from your requests that you are helpless and that your friend is strong and kind. You glorify your friend by needing and counting on that person and asking him or her for help.

In John 15:5 Jesus says: "I am the vine, you are the branches; he who abides in Me and I in him, he bears much fruit, for apart from Me you can do nothing" (NASB). So we really are paralyzed. Without Christ we are not capable of doing anything. But according to John 15:5 God intends for us to do great things—namely, bear fruit.

How then do we glorify him? Jesus gives the answer in verse 7: "If you abide in Me, and My words abide in you, ask whatever you wish, and it will be done for you" (NASB). Thus we pray! We ask God to do for us through Christ what we can't do for ourselves—bear fruit. Verse 8 gives the result: "By this is My Father glorified, that you bear much fruit" (NASB). So how is God glorified by prayer? Prayer is the open admission that without Christ we can do nothing. And prayer is the turning away from ourselves to God in the confidence that He will provide the help that we need. Prayer humbles us as needy, and exalts God as wealthy. Failure in our prayer life generally reflects our failure to know Jesus. "If you knew who was talking to you, you would ask me!" A prayerless Christian is like having your room wallpapered with Nordstrom gift certificates but always shopping at Wal-Mart because you don't know any better.

And the implication is that those who do ask—Christians who spend time in prayer—do it because they see that God is a great giver and that Christ is wise and merciful and powerful beyond measure. And therefore their prayer glorifies Christ and honors His Father. The chief end of humanity is to glorify God. Therefore, when we become what God created us to be we become people of prayer.

Prayer is the essential activity of waiting upon God: acknowledging our helplessness and His power, calling upon Him for help, seeking His counsel. So it is evident why God so often commands prayer, since His purpose in the world is to be exalted for His mercy. Prayer is the antidote for the disease of self-confidence that opposes God's goal of receiving glory by working for those who wait for Him.

PRAYER IS SEEKING GOD'S COMPANIONSHIP

You don't have to live long to discover that God created people to thrive on companionship. Children love to play with friends, and adolescents enjoy socializing. Adults maintain relationships with friends and colleagues and make lifetime commitments to a spouse and children. No matter how many or how deep your friendships, however, at some point you begin to realize that human companionship is not enough. Even the best of friends can't be with you all the time. They move away, fade away, or die. Sometimes unable to understand what you are going through, they aren't always faithful and dependable. If you try to meet all your companionship needs through human beings, you are doomed to perpetual, unfulfilled yearnings.

But God does not expect us to have only human friends. Proverbs 18:24 declares: "There is a friend who sticks closer than a brother" (NIV). Hebrews 4:15 tells us that Jesus, having been "tempted in every way, just as we are" (NIV), understands us completely. Psalm 121:3 assures us that our divine friend is always available to us: "He who watches over you will not slumber" (NIV).

Your heavenly Friend always listens. He freely communicates with you with no barriers. When He expresses affection, He means it. He is patient with your immaturity, forgives you when you wrong Him, and stays committed to you even when you ignore Him for long periods of time. He is always faithful.

PRAYER IS SEEKING GOD'S CONFIDENCE

Companionship is wonderful. Even more wonderful is realizing who your closest companion is—God, the creator and sustainer of the universe, able to empower you to face anything that comes your way.

Some summers ago at a Christian camp I wanted to learn to sail a sailboat. So a friend of mine took me out to the deep part of the lake to teach me how. It was very easy. Very easy, that is, when he did it. But when I tried to maneuver the boat alone, I discovered how hard it actually was. I kept tipping the boat again and again. But with my friend on board, I had both companionship and confidence.

As you enjoy God's presence in your life, you become increasingly aware of your companion's identity and power and character. Nothing is too difficult for God to handle. His power has no limits. Life can't throw anything at you that you can't handle with God.

You may be experiencing clear sailing right now. Having the all-powerful God as your companion may not seem very important. But your life will not be free of storms for long. You are going to have your share of heartbreak, disappointment, trial, and tragedy. But with God's presence in your life, you will be able to face such storms with confidence.

The more you know God, the more at peace you should be. Yes, negative circumstances do come, and they can throw you off balance. If you are not at peace—if you do not experience a growing sense of inner peace—it's because your knowledge of God is not increasing. When you experience the presence of God, He can enable you to sleep in troubled waters. Should you have no money, you know that it's not the last word. If your enemies move against you, you understand that they will not make the final decision about your fate. And should people reject you, you can say, "No, I'm never alone." The presence of God comforts the heart, because He dictates the final circumstances.

Jesus said to His disciples and to us:

"So I say to you: Ask and it will be given to you; seek and you will find; knock and the door will be opened to you. For everyone who asks receives; he who seeks finds; and to him who knocks, the door will be opened. Which of you fathers, if his son asks for a fish, will give him a snake instead? Or if he asks for an egg, will give him a scorpion? If you then, though you are evil, know how to give good gifts to your children, how much more will your Father in heaven give the Holy Spirit to those who ask him!" (Luke 11:9-13, NIV).

PRAYER IS SEEKING GOD'S COMPASSION

The more time you spend with Christ, the more you begin to act like Him. People matter to Jesus, and what is important to Him is also important to His followers. His concern and compassion begin to rub off on you. Look at what happened to the apostle John. At one point he wanted to destroy a whole city because some of its residents didn't want Jesus to stay there (Luke 9:54). After a lifetime in God's presence, however, he wrote: "Whoever does not love does not know God, because God is love" (1 John 4:8, NIV). Or consider Peter, the apostle who—even after Pentecost—couldn't bear to associate with certain people (Gal. 2:11-14). In his famous "ladder" of Christian virtues he shows how Christlike character develops: "Add to your faith goodness; and to goodness, knowledge; and to knowledge, self-control; and to self-control, perseverance; and to perseverance, godliness; and to godliness, brotherly kindness; and to brotherly kindness, love" (2 Peter 1:5-7, NIV). Through his lifelong association with Christ, Peter came to value brotherly kindness and love. He knew that it is God who helps us to grow in "brotherly kindness" and at the same time makes us aware of His presence through the compassion and love of other Christians.

When we live in constant communion with God, we find our needs met, our faith increased, and our love expanded. We begin to feel God's peace in our hearts, and experience the joy of His worship.

If you hang around radioactive material, it's going to do something to you. And if you remain in the presence of God, it will also affect you. God will change you. He is in the business of transforming people.

PRAYER IS SEEKING GOD'S POWER

John 15:5-8 tells us: "I am the vine; you are the branches. If a man remains in me and I in him, he will bear much fruit; apart from me you can do nothing. If anyone does not remain in me, he is like a branch that is thrown away and withers; such branches are picked up, thrown into the fire and burned. If you remain in me and my words remain in you, ask whatever you wish, and it will be given you. This is to my Father's glory, that you bear much fruit, showing yourselves to be my disciples" (NIV).

An old farmer walked into the tool department at the local hardware store.

"May I help you?" the clerk asked.

"I'm lookin' for a new saw, young man."

"Just what kind of saw do you need? What do you plan to use it for?"

The old man scratched his head. "Well, I suppose I'll be needin' it mainly for cuttin' firewood."

"Right over here," the clerk said as he led the man through the aisles. "This," he said, pointing to a chain saw, "would be just what you need."

"Never did use one of those," the old man told him. "Is it faster than a handsaw?"

"There's no comparison. In fact, I bet you could saw 20 trees with this chain saw in the time it would take you to saw one with a handsaw."

So the old farmer bought the chain saw and left the store. Two weeks later the clerk saw, to his surprise, the man back with the chain saw in hand.

"Well, what do you think?" the clerk asked.

"It's the worst saw I've ever used. I've been tryin' to cut down one tree for almost two weeks. And I'm still cuttin'. I'm returnin' this and buyin' myself a handsaw."

"Let me take a look at it," said the clerk as he picked up the chain saw. Stepping back from the counter, he yanked the starter rope, and the saw roared into action.

The old farmer nearly jumped from under his straw hat. "Whoa! Where did that noise come from?"*

When we don't pray, our lives are like the old farmer's. We operate and live depending on our own human resources, talents, and power. Yet the power of the Holy Spirit, which can do the impossible, is available to us by a strong connection with God. The intensity of our worship is in direct proportion to the intensity of our prayer life. Worship is giving God His worth. It is attributing to Him His power.

AN APPEAL

One of the main reasons that so many of us don't have a significant prayer life is not so much that we don't want to, but that we don't plan to. If you want to take a four-week vacation, you don't just get up one summer morning and say, "Hey, let's go today!" You won't have anything ready or know where to go. Nothing has been planned.

That is how many of us treat prayer. We get up day after day and realize that significant times of prayer should be a part of our life, but nothing's ever done about it. Nothing has been planned. And most of us recognize that the opposite of planning is not a wonderful flow of deep, spontaneous experiences in prayer. Rather, the opposite of planning is the rut. If you don't plan a vacation, you will probably just stay home and watch TV. The natural, unplanned flow of spiritual life sinks to the lowest ebb of vitality.

If you want renewal in your life of prayer, you must *plan* to see it.

Therefore, my simple exhortation is this: Let us take time this very day to rethink our priorities and how prayer fits into them. Make some new resolves. Try some new ventures with God. Set a time and a place for it to happen. Don't be tyrannized by the press of busy days. We all need mid-course corrections. Make this a day of turning to prayer—for the glory of God and for the fullness of your life.

A friend of mine once said, "I don't need another book on prayer. I know enough about prayer. I simply must take time to pray. Because we will never find time, we must seize it."

Let me encourage you to give your life back to God at a deeper level—a level at which you seek His help to fulfill your responsibility. Commit yourself more deeply to the Lord, pray for His aid, and begin to experience His good helping hand daily. I have learned that prayer is more of an attitude than a posture or a form of expression. It is a manifestation of dependence on God. Through prayer I realize that I am not sufficient in myself and need help. I can't do it, but God can enable me do it. As the songs say, "I need Thee every hour" and I am "learning to lean." Our whole life, when we live it to the glory of God, can be a form of prayer. We learn to lean on Jesus throughout every day, depending upon Him for help to live a supernatural life in a tough, worldly environment. It is like praying "without ceasing" (1 Thess. 5:17).

I challenge you to respond to God, to get to know Him. It will demand effort. You may have to get up a little earlier so that you can spend time in His Word and time on your knees. In addition, you'll need to spend time with His people and time in His presence, because our great God deserves a response.

---

*See Renée Kempf Coffee, *The Official 1993 Devotional Book for Super Kids* (Hagerstown, Md.: Review and Herald Pub. Assn., 1992), p. 118.

"For the word of God is living and active. Sharper than any double-edged sword, it penetrates even to dividing soul and spirit, joints and marrow; it judges the thoughts and attitudes of the heart" (Heb. 4:12, NIV).

". . . who have tasted the goodness of the word of God and the powers of the coming age" (Heb. 6:5, NIV).

"The grass withers and the flowers fall, but the word of our God stands forever" (Isa. 40:8, NIV).

6

The Word of God and Worship

EZRA THE SCRIBE

We can trace the use of God's Word in worship back to the beginnings of corporate worship at Mount Sinai. Nevertheless, it was the emphasis of Ezra the scribe that made Scripture central to Jewish public worship. Ezra was a Babylonian Jew who went to the Holy Land as the head of the second wave of immigrants after the Exile. When to his shock he discovered the weak spiritual condition of the people of Jerusalem (spiritual apathy always accompanies a lack of emphasis on the Word of God), he rent his garments, fasted, and prayed for renewal. Then, under his leadership, far-reaching reforms began, including renewal of worship. Scripture records its restoration in the following words: "Ezra opened the book. All the people could see him because he was standing above them; and as he opened it, the people all stood up. Ezra praised the Lord, the great God; and all the people lifted their hands and responded, 'Amen! Amen!' Then they bowed down and worshiped the Lord with their faces to the ground.

"The Levites . . . instructed the people in the Law while the people were standing there. They read from the Book of the Law of God, making it clear and giving the meaning so that the people could understand what was being read" (Neh. 8:5-8, NIV).

It is interesting to note all that is going on in this incident: the reader standing in a place everyone could see him; the people standing as Ezra opened the book, lifting their hands and saying "Amen." Then, as the Levites read the Word of God and explained its meaning, the people, moved by the Spirit of God, bowed to the ground in an act of worship and commitment. Here was no passive mumbling of Scripture, no mere act of seeking information! Reading Scripture was an act of worship that led to reexamination of life and to transformation.

The Bible provides the parameters of our worship, telling us how to worship, whom to worship, the purpose of worship, and the power of our worship.

The Word Reveals to Us the God We Worship

THE NATURE AND CHARACTER OF GOD

The Bible reveals what kind of God we worship. Psalm 145:5 declares, "On the glorious splendor of Your majesty and on Your wonderful works, I will meditate" (NASB), and in the remainder of the chapter the psalmist does just that. He mentions specifically God's greatness, His mighty acts, His power, His goodness, His righteousness, His grace, His mercy, His compassion, His graciousness, His loving-kindness, His holiness, His glory, His sovereignty, His sustaining power, and His nearness to those who call upon Him. In short, the author focuses on God's attributes.

Well, what do we do with such divine attributes?

When Scripture gets read in church (or, for that matter, at home) and then the interpretation comes through the sermon or other means, we can react in several ways. One involves analyzing the content of Scripture purely for historical and theological information. Another way is to relate it to the life of someone else. But the right thing to do is to ask ourselves, "What is God saying to me today? How does He want to transform my life? What is it in my life that needs change? Where do I need to grow? Or where in my experience do I require more trust?" I have discovered during the years that God, as through His Word He reveals His character, His attributes, and His acts, is leading me to a higher experience with Him. For instance, when the Word unveils God's holiness, I see it as a brilliant white light focusing on me, making my sins stand out as intolerable stains. Such an encounter, coupled with the experience of His love, often moved me to confess my sins and renew my commitment to Him. I was able to see myself in the light of His perfection. Now, whenever I think of divine holiness, I am immediately reminded of who I am—a sinner who desperately needs the cleansing that comes only from Christ.

What we have to remember is to make the right decision. I gave a friend of mine a Bible some time ago and urged him to read it. He came to me a few weeks later and gave it back to me. "This book requires too many changes, and I am not willing to make them," he said. "Not yet, anyway."

Let us say that you go to a specialty store and find that it stocks a microscope. After examining it and discovering how strong the lenses are, you soon find yourself fascinated by its powerful ability to let you see things that you do not perceive ordinarily. So you decide to purchase it and take it home. Looking through its lens to study crystals and the petals of flowers, you become amazed at their beauty and detail. You thoroughly enjoy using it until one day you examine some food you were planning to eat for dinner. Much to your dismay, you discover that tiny living creatures are crawling in it. Since you are especially fond of this particular food, you wonder what to do. Finally, you conclude that there is only one way out of your dilemma—you will destroy the instrument that has revealed the distasteful fact. So you smash the microscope to pieces!

"How foolish!" you say. But many people do the same thing with the Word of God. They hate it and would like to get rid of it because it reveals their evil nature. Here is another example illustrating how we should react to Scripture and its interpretation: Isaiah 40:26 tells us that God created the stars, and called them by name, and that "because of the greatness of His might and the strength of His power, not one of them is missing" (NASB). God has displayed His power by filling the sky with stars.

As I focus on His power and greatness, I find myself filled with wonder that the God whose power hung the stars in space could reach down, in infinite love, and care for me. Why does such a God love me at all? I don't know why, but He does. And my experience of the God of all power has brought me back to a wonderful appreciation of the God of all love, and that now drives me to bow down in submission, adoration, and worship.

THE NATURE AND CHARACTER OF JESUS CHRIST

The Bible focuses not only on the character and nature of God, but also on the character of Jesus Christ. Paul's desire for the Christians at Colossae was "that their hearts may be encouraged, having been knit together in love, and attaining to all the wealth that comes from the full assurance of understanding, resulting in a true knowledge of God's mystery, that is, *Christ Himself, in whom are hidden all the treasures of wisdom and knowledge*" (Col. 2:2, 3, NASB).

Nothing will lead our hearts to worship more readily than knowing *who* Jesus is and *what* He has done for us. I have a poster in my office with a list of many of the names given to Jesus in Scripture. Just a quick reading through it provides a wealth of worship material. Consider a few of His names: Advocate, Almighty, Bread of Life, Bridegroom, Chief Cornerstone, Counselor, Deliverer, Door, Good Teacher, Great Shepherd, Holy One of God, King Eternal, King of Glory, Lamb of God, Life, Light, Messiah, Prince of Peace, Redeemer, Rock, Savior, Truth, Way, Wonderful, Word of Life.

Christ Jesus is *all* of these and so much more. Think for a moment what it means to know that Jesus is our Great Shepherd. He guides us on the path of righteousness, protects us from evil, leads us to spiritual refreshment, and provides for us the refuge of His presence. He has even laid down His life on our behalf.

Or consider what it means to know that Jesus is the Truth, that we have no need to seek elsewhere for absolutes or for wisdom. In Him we have "all the treasures of wisdom and knowledge" (Col. 2:3, NASB).

Or take Jesus as the Deliverer. Meditate on all that He has rescued you from—fear, loneliness, condemnation, confusion, frustration; and all that He has given you in exchange—peace, freedom, eternal life, fellowship with God, joy, love, and meaningful service.

A story tells about a teenage boy who was deeply interested in scientific subjects, especially astronomy. So his father bought him a very expensive telescope. Since the young fellow had studied the principles of optics, he found the instrument to be most intriguing. He took it apart, examined the lenses, and made detailed calculations on the distance of its point of focus. The youth became so absorbed in gaining a technical knowledge of the telescope itself that he never got around to looking at the stars. Although he knew a lot about that fine instrument, he missed seeing the wonders of the heavens.

God has a higher goal for the Bible than for Christians just to know all the facts and figures contained in it. Its purpose is that we might see God and His Son, Jesus Christ, and know Them.

Surely in the work and ministry of Jesus we can find much cause for worship. We know Christ through the Bible, and we understand the Bible through the knowledge of Christ and the Spirit that He sent.

The Word Reveals to Us the Purpose of Our Worship

THE WORD IS THE MEANS OF THE OPERATION OF THE HOLY SPIRIT

God commands us to be filled with the Holy Spirit: "Do not get drunk on wine, which leads to debauchery. Instead, be filled with the Spirit" (Eph. 5:18, NIV). How does the Spirit come? In Galatians 3:2 Paul asks, "Did you receive the Spirit by the works of the Law, or by hearing with faith?" (NASB). The answer, of course, is "hearing with faith." Hearing what? The Word of God!

The Spirit inspired the Word and therefore He goes where the Word goes. The more of God's Word that you know and love, the more of God's Spirit that you will experience. Instead of drinking wine we should drink the Spirit. How? By setting our minds on the things of the Spirit: "Those who live according to the Spirit, the things of the Spirit" (Rom. 8:5, NKJV).

What are the things of the Spirit? The teachings of Scripture. We drink in the Spirit by focusing our minds on the things of the Spirit, namely the

Word of God. And the fruit of the Spirit is true worship. Jesus said, "Those who worship Him must worship in spirit and truth" (John 4:24, NKJV).

THE WORD GIVES HOPE

It does not take much intelligence to recognize that the world's greatest need today is for hope. Sometimes faith and hope are virtual synonyms in Scripture. "Faith is the assurance of things *hoped* for" (Heb. 11:1, NASB). Without this hope for the future we get discouraged and depressed, and our joy drains away. Hope is absolutely essential to Christian worship. We worship a God who gives us hope and direction.

And how do we maintain hope? The psalmist puts it like this: "He established a testimony in Jacob, and appointed a law in Israel, which He commanded our fathers, that they should make them known to their children . . . that they may set their *hope* in God" (Ps. 78:5-7, NKJV). In other words, the "testimony" and the "law"—the Word of God—create the hope that we so desperately need.

Paul puts it so plainly: "Whatever things were written before were written for our learning, that we through the patience and comfort of the Scriptures might have *hope*" (Rom. 15:4, NKJV). The whole Bible has as its aim and power to create hope in the hearts of God's people. And when hope abounds, worship fills the heart.

THE WORD SHALL MAKE YOU FREE

Another essential element of worship is freedom. None of us would be able to worship if we were not free from what we hate and free for what we love. And where do we find true freedom? Psalm 119:45 states: "I will walk at liberty, for I seek Your precepts" (NKJV). The picture is one of open spaces. The Word frees us from smallness of mind (1 Kings 4:29) and from threatening confinements (Ps. 18:19). Jesus says, "You shall know the truth, and the truth shall make you *free*" (John 8:32, NKJV). The freedom He has in mind is deliverance from the slavery of sin (verse 34). Or, to put it positively, it is freedom for holiness. The promises of God's grace provide the power that makes the demands of God's holiness an experience of freedom rather than fear. "By which have been given to us exceedingly great and precious promises, that through these you may be partakers of the divine nature" (2 Peter 1:4, NKJV; cf. John 15:3). Freed from corruption, freed to share the likeness of God—by the precious and very great promises! Therefore, we should pray for each other the way Jesus prays for us in John 17:17: "Sanctify them in the truth; Your word is truth" (NASB). "Pursue peace with all people, and holiness, without which no one will see the Lord" (Heb. 12:14, NKJV). How important, then, is the truth that sanctifies! "Your word is a lamp to my feet and a light to my path" (Ps. 119:105, NASB). "Your word I have hidden in my heart, that I might not sin against You" (Ps. 119:11, NKJV).

Mark Twain once said: "Most people are bothered by those passages of Scripture they do not understand, but the passages that bother me most are those I do understand."

Navigators keep oceangoing ships on course by what is known as the "celestial fix." With the instruments fixed on the stars, they can tell exactly where they are on the trackless ocean, and whether or not they need to correct their course.

Believers need a "celestial fix" on God for daily guidance. Proverbs 15:3 reminds us that "the eyes of the Lord are in every place, keeping watch on the evil and the good" (NKJV). His gaze scans like a surveillance camera. When we tune in daily with open hearts, desiring direction, He will show us where we are and guide us back on course if we have drifted away.

Before God gave the Ten Commandments to Israel, He freed them so they might worship Him.

THE WORD REVEALS TO US THE POWER OF OUR WORSHIP

More than a collection of words on pages, the Bible is *God-breathed*. Divine authority and power are present in every word and can penetrate into the deepest parts of our being. God describes His Word as a *seed*, a *sword*, a *hammer*, and *fire*. Multitudes, from kings to peasants, have had their lives radically changed through the Word. Through the Bible God speaks to us by the power of His Spirit.

FAITH COMES BY HEARING THE WORD OF GOD

The Word of God begets and sustains spiritual *life* because it begets and sustains *faith*. "These have been written," John says, "so that you may *believe* that Jesus is the Christ, the Son of God; and that *believing* you may have *life* in His name" (John 20:31, NASB). "Faith comes by hearing," writes the apostle Paul, "and hearing by the word of God" (Rom. 10:17, NKJV). The faith that starts our life in Christ and by which we go on living comes from hearing the Word of God.

Our spiritual life begins by the Word of God: "Of His own will He brought us forth by the word of truth" (James 1:18, NKJV). "Having been born again, . . . through the word of God which lives and abides forever" (1 Peter 1:23, NKJV).

The Bible is as necessary to our spiritual life as oxygen is to sustain our physical existence. Not only do we *begin* to live by God's Word, but we also *go on* living by it: "Man shall not live by bread alone, but by every word that proceeds from the mouth of God" (Matt. 4:4, NKJV; cf. Deut. 8:3). Our physical life is created and upheld by the Word of God, and our spiritual life is quickened and sustained by the Word of God.

Indeed, the Bible is the source of our life—physical as well as spiritual—all because of the power of the Word of God. Therefore, knowing that God is the source of my existence leads me to a life of worship and adoration.

The Word of God gives birth to and sustains faith, and out of faith grows meaningful worship.

THE EVIL ONE IS OVERCOME BY THE WORD OF GOD

Satan's number one objective is to destroy our worship. We have one offensive weapon: the sword of the Spirit, the Word of God (Eph. 6:17). But what many Christians fail to realize is that we can't draw the sword from someone else's scabbard. When we don't wear it, we can't wield it. If the Word of God does not abide in us (John 15:7) we will reach for it in vain when the enemy strikes. But if we do wear it—if it lives within us—what mighty warriors we can be! "I have written to you, young men, because you are strong, and the word of God abides in you, and you have overcome the evil one" (1 John 2:14, NASB).

Nearly 2,000 years ago Satan engaged our Lord in deadly combat in the wilderness of Judea. In similar struggles through the centuries against scores of brave Christian warriors, Satan has launched waves of fierce attacks, winning a skirmish here and there, but always losing in the end. Defeat has seemingly not discouraged him. He continues still to fight the people of God at every turn.

Let us then look together at Jesus' great battle with Satan. As we learn how He fought the devil, let us be empowered in the same manner.

"Then Jesus was led by the Spirit into the desert to be tempted by the devil. After fasting forty days and forty nights, he was hungry. The tempter came to him and said, 'If you are the Son of God, tell these stones to become bread.'

"Jesus answered, 'It is written: "Man does not live on bread alone, but on every word that comes from the mouth of God."'

"Then the devil took him to the holy city and had him stand on the highest point of the temple. 'If you are the Son of God,' he said, 'throw yourself down. For it is written: "He will command his angels concerning you, and they will lift you up in their hands, so that you will not strike your foot against a stone."'

"Jesus answered him, 'It is also written: "Do not put the Lord your God to the test."'

"Again, the devil took him to a very high mountain and showed him all the kingdoms of the world and their splendor. 'All this I will give you,' he said, 'if you will bow down and worship me.'

"Jesus said to him, 'Away from me, Satan! For it is written: "Worship the Lord your God, and serve him only."'

"Then the devil left him, and angels came and attended him" (Matt. 4:1-11, NIV).

Matthew 4 presents one of the greatest scenes of combat in all of human history. The struggle was unique not because of the technology of the armaments or the number of combatants, but rather because the battle's outcome would determine the destiny of the world and of every human being, including you and me. Satan was truly prepared for his conflict with Jesus. Because he had meticulously honed his arguments and rehearsed his strategy, his arsenal was ready. Jesus also was set for battle. It was He who chose the weapon employed in the conflict. The most powerful one that the world has ever seen, it dwarfs even our great nuclear arsenals of today. That weapon is the Word of God.

The same great weapon of warfare that He so expertly used, our heavenly Father graciously gives us today. It worked for Jesus, for Luther, for Wesley and Moody, and it will do its task perfectly for you and me, also. It never fails.

Human beings may try to eradicate the Word, and Satan may attempt to choke it out, but the Bible will stand. The fact that the Bible is alive and life-giving gives it both power and longevity, "The word of God is living and active. Sharper than any double-edged sword, it penetrates even to dividing soul and spirit, joints and marrow; it judges the thoughts and attitudes of the heart" (Heb. 4:12, NIV).

God's Word is personal, practical, and powerful. The Bible is a book of hope. While it may disturb and shake you to your foundations, it will always comfort you and enable you. Surely Matthew 4 is written for our instruction. Jesus could have chosen and used many weapons. He might have responded by calling a legion of angels to trample Satan underfoot. Or He could have been transfigured before that rascal and proved His divinity on the spot. But instead Jesus, in His full humanity, to identify with you and me, chose to use the Word of God. It was His common practice. All through His earthly ministry He spoke about and employed the living Word of God. When He taught, He taught Scripture. And when He shared about Himself, His resurrection, and His coming again, He did so through the Scriptures. The Word of God was constantly on His lips. So it ought to be for us. "I have hidden your word in my heart" (Ps. 119:11, NIV).

AN EARNEST EXHORTATION

The Bible as the Word of God is the source of life and faith and power and hope and freedom and wisdom and comfort and assurance and victory over our greatest enemy. Is it any wonder, then, that those who knew best said, "The precepts of the Lord are right, *rejoicing* the heart" (Ps. 19:8, NASB)? "I will *delight* myself in thy statutes: I will not forget thy word" (Ps. 119:16).

Let us labor to memorize the Word of God—for worship and for warfare. If we do not carry it in our heads, we cannot savor it in our hearts or wield it in the Spirit. Should you go out without the kindling of the Word of God, the fire of Christian worship will be quenched before midmorning.

Worship is when the Lord God would come down to the Garden of Eden to commune with Adam and Eve (see Gen. 3:8, 9). Therefore, worship is, quite simply, walking and talking with the Lord. God has always ordained it to be more than a monologue of my telling Him how I feel about Him. And it is more than just my talking to God—it is also His speaking to me! It is two-way communication.

Some have called worship the "language of love." When we worship, we express our love to God. But love must flow as an exchange between two individuals. There must be give and take, talking and listening, transmitting and receiving. Thus worship must contain both elements in order to be complete. First it must consist of our expressions to God through praise, offering, and prayer, and then it must also include listening to His responses through the Word.

Mortimer J. Adler, in *How to Read a Book,* has observed that the one time people read for all they are worth is when they are in love and are reading a love letter. Devouring every word, they read between the lines and in the margins. Furthermore, they read the whole in terms of the parts, and each part in terms of the whole. As a result, they grow sensitive to context and ambiguity, to insinuation and implication. They perceive the color of words, the order of phrases, and the weight of sentences. Sometimes they may even take the punctuation into account. Above all, they read carefully and in depth.

So should believers read the "love letter" that the Eternal Lover has given to us so that we may better know Him and His purpose.

7

Praise and Worship

THE ESSENCE OF PRAISE

Praise is not a difficult concept to understand, for it is part of our everyday lives. We "praise" our children when they please us, employees for a job well done, and dogs when they perform tricks nicely. But above and beyond all that, praise is something that we direct toward God or something we express to others about Him. Some of the definitions for "praise" in the dictionary highlight its simplicity: "to commend; to applaud; to express approval or admiration of; to extol in words or in song; to magnify; to glorify." Notice the bidirectional focus of praise inherent in these definitions: we praise God directly by extolling Him or expressing our admiration of Him. On the other hand, we praise God indirectly by commending Him or magnifying Him to others. Praise can be given directly to God, or it can be expressed to others in reference to Him.

Preoccupied with who God is and what He has done, praise focuses on both His incomparable character and His wondrous acts on behalf of His children. When God does something glorious for us, we love to lift high His praises. And yet praise is not simply our thankful response to His provision. It is also very fitting even when we have no specific gift of God in mind. He is worthy to be praised solely for who He is.

Many times praise is a function of the will. We must decide and determine to praise the Lord, even when we do not feel like it. Praise is not contingent upon our feelings—it is based upon God's inherent greatness, and that never changes! Notice how David spoke: "Bless the Lord, O my soul; and all that is within me, bless His holy name" (Ps 103:1, NKJV). Sometimes we are down in the dumps or dry spiritually, and it is at these times that we must say, "Bless the Lord!" Praise must function according to our will and not our emotions.

"But how can I praise," you may ask, "when I feel completely depressed or deflated emotionally?" We can find an answer in the Psalms, for they were written by individuals who, like us, experienced deep emotional valleys. One psalmist described his feelings in this way: "My soul is downcast within me." So he asked himself: "Why are you downcast, O my soul? Why so disturbed within me?" Then he proceeded to get tough on himself: "Put your hope in God." His next statement so beautifully shows the discipline of praise: *"For I will yet praise him"* (Ps. 42:5, NIV). The Lord wants all of us to come to that same point at which we determine to praise Him regardless of our feelings and circumstances.

I have experienced this many times in my life. Rather than giving in to discouragement, I start praising the Lord and remembering His acts both in history and in my life. The result is pure joy. God is great, and greatly He is to be praised.

WHY SHOULD WE PRAISE THE LORD?

First of all, we praise Him because His Word commands us to do so. "Praise ye the Lord" (Ps. 150:1). "Why does God demand our praise?" you may ask. "Is He some sort of egomaniac who feeds off our adulation?" No, it is not that God requires our praises, but He knows that we need to praise

Him! God has commanded praise for our own good. Not until we praise Him are we able to come into proper relationship with Him. Without a thankful and praising heart, we will never grow in the grace of Christ Jesus. God is enthroned in our praise (see Ps. 22:3, NASB). He is so pleased with our praise that He literally surrounds Himself with it.

Second, praise has power in it. When we stop trying to fight our battles and simply begin to praise the God who has said that He will fight for us, He is free to release His power and provision on our behalf. Praise is our weapon in spiritual warfare. It will bring victory, deliverance, and blessing.

Perhaps the most dramatic illustration of praise and worship appears in Jehoshaphat's confrontation with the Moabites and the Ammonites, as recorded in 2 Chronicles 20. The first step the king took was to call a fast and gather the people together for prayer. In that prayer Jehoshaphat reminded the Lord of His promises and His past interventions in behalf of the people of Israel. The result was a Spirit-given message from the priest Jahaziel that God would give them the victory. The next day the king assembled the people for battle, but he did a strange thing: he put the singers ahead of the soldiers! "And when he had consulted with the people, he appointed those who should sing to the Lord, and who should praise the beauty of holiness, as they went out before the army and were saying: 'Praise the Lord, for His mercy endures forever'" (verse 21, NKJV).

What was the result? God caused the invading armies to defeat each other! Jehoshaphat and his people did not need to fight at all! They simply claimed the spoils and returned to Jerusalem for a great praise service at the Temple.

When the enemy surrounded Israel, the first thing Jehoshaphat did was to get the choir to sing praises to God. Praise defeated the invaders. Israel did not have to do anything. They had no need to fight, because the Lord did it for them. The battle belongs to the Lord. Praise and celebration has great power in it. Let us live a life of praise, celebration, and thanksgiving.

Our human tendency, when facing a crisis, is to defend ourselves through our own efforts—or perhaps, when we see we cannot possibly overcome, to run to God and beg for His protection. While He wants us to come to Him for deliverance, we should do it the way of Jehoshaphat and his army, with songs of praise instead of fearful and tearful pleas. He honors the faith that praises Him before the battle is won, not just afterward.

So when you face difficult times, do what James says. Have a party, invite your friends, and in advance rejoice in the Lord, and God will take care of the rest (James 1:2-8).

A third reason for praising God is simply that He is worthy of it. "Great is the Lord, and greatly to be praised" (Ps. 48:1, NKJV). "Thou art worthy O Lord, to receive glory and honour and power: for thou hast created all things, and for thy pleasure they are and were created" (Rev. 4:11). Consider these beautiful words of Martin Luther: "A person cannot praise God only, unless he understands that there is nothing in himself worthy of praise, but that all that is worthy of praise is of God and from God. But since God is eternally praiseworthy, because He is the infinite God and can never be exhausted, therefore they will praise Him for ever and ever."[1]

When we truly sense God's greatness, praise comes easily. One delightful way to concentrate on God's character is to study the divine names. Old Testament praise occupied itself with the name of God. "I will praise your name, O Lord, for it is good" (Ps. 54:6, NKJV). "Oh, magnify the Lord with me, and let us exalt His name together" (Ps. 34:3, NKJV). The Hebrews praised God's name, because for them a person's name indicated an individual's character. I remember that the people in the Middle East, where I grew up, would even wait a few years to name their children so that they could choose names in keeping with the children's personalities and character. God liked that ancient custom and decided to reveal His character to the Israelites by giving them a variety of names for Himself.

It is what happened in Exodus 15:26, when the Lord said, in essence, "You can call me 'Jehovah-raphah,' because I am the Lord who heals you!" In Genesis 22 God reveals Himself as "Jehovah-jireh" when He wanted to show that He would provide for His people. And in the last verse of the book of Ezekiel God gave His name as "Jehovah-shammah," which means "The Lord is there" (Eze. 48:35). God was revealing His omnipresence—He will never leave us or forsake us! It is appropriate, therefore, for praise to focus on all that the various names of God in Scripture represent.

Fourth, we were created to praise Him. Humanity's chief end is to glorify God and to enjoy Him forever, a fact clearly brought out in Scripture. Jeremiah 13:11 shows us that God called the house of Israel to Himself specifically for His praise, a reality echoed in 1 Peter 2:9: "But you are a chosen generation, a royal priesthood, a holy nation, His own special people, that you may proclaim the praises of Him who called you out of darkness into His marvelous light" (NKJV). God has chosen us for the express purpose of declaring His praises! Isaiah capsulated this so beautifully: "This people I have formed for Myself; they shall declare My praise" (Isa. 43:21, NKJV).

Many people today long for fulfillment and search desperately for it in all the wrong places. They will never find complete fulfillment in their innermost beings until they come into proper relationship with God through praise. A. W. Tozer has said: "The purpose of God in sending His Son to die and rise and live and be at the right hand of God the Father was that He might restore to us the missing jewel, the jewel of worship; that we might come back and learn to do again that which we were created to do in the first place—worship the Lord in the beauty of holiness."[2]

Praise should not be a difficult task to master, but it should flow from our lives in a most natural way, for it is, in fact, a normal tendency inherent within our very fiber, placed there purposely by our Creator and Father.

WHEN SHOULD WE PRAISE?

Israel experienced God's deliverance time and time again. They received blessing after blessing from Him, but they quickly forgot what He had done for them. Instead of offering praise, they responded with complaints (see Ps. 105; 106).

We are told that if we praised God every time we had evidence of His love and care for us, we would be continually praising Him. It's so easy instead to take His blessings for granted, isn't it?

Scripture invites us to praise Him in good times—and in bad times. We don't have to wait to praise God until something good happens. The Bible urges us to praise Him when things are going wrong. Praise the Lord whether you feel it like it or not. Praise the Lord even when you fall into darkness or things are not going your way. Praise Him even in temptation. Praise the Lord always, under all circumstances, and in all situations.

But why would you want to praise God when things go wrong? What can you find to praise Him about then?

A story tells of an old preacher walking to town one day who met a robber who took all that he had. That evening he wrote in his diary, "Today I was robbed, and I praise God for the following reasons: first, that

I have never been robbed before. Second, that although he took my money, he did not take my life. Third, that although he took all I had, it wasn't much! And fourth, I am thankful that it was I who was robbed, and not I who robbed."

Even in the darkest times of our lives, we can be thankful both for the light that we have had before and for the light that we are promised up ahead. And we can be thankful for the one who stays with us, even in the darkness. We may not be able to sense His presence, but we can know that He's there.

The point is this: we are to praise the Lord constantly. "I will bless the Lord at all times: his praise shall continually be in my mouth" (Ps. 34:1). No matter what time of day it is, and regardless of where we find ourselves, it is always fitting to bless the Lord.

But is it appropriate to praise the Lord in the hard times, when everything is going wrong? The answer resounds from the hills: *Yes!* The Old Testament prophet Habakkuk gave his remedy for disastrous times:

"Though the fig tree may not blossom
  nor fruit be on the vines;
  though the labor of the olive may fail,
  and the fields yield no food;
  though the flock may be cut off from the fold,
  and there be no herd in the stalls—
  yet I will rejoice in the Lord,
  I will joy in the God of my salvation" (Hab. 3:17, 18, NKJV).

A modern rendition of this passage might read like this:
"Though the economy is unstable,
  and unemployment is rising,
  though Communism may be growing,
  and terrorism is rampant,
   though the car is broken down and my wife is
  stranded downtown,
  though my kid just broke his arm and the medical
  insurance ran out,
  yet I will rejoice in the Lord,
  I will be joyful in God my Savior!"[3]

It is not hypocritical to praise the Lord in hard times—that is precisely when we need to lift our voices in praise to God! It is God's will that we offer up thanks in every situation in which we find ourselves.

HOW SHOULD WE PRAISE THE LORD?

Praise can come in countless forms. If you are looking for as many ways as possible to make your experience of praise a delight, perhaps you will want to consider some of the methods others have used in their worship of God.

We can praise God in song. Singing is probably the most common form of praise we employ today. "Let the high praises of God be in their mouth, and a two-edged sword in their hand" (Ps. 149:6, NKJV). Paul and Silas used this method when they were in jail. Do you remember the result? God responded to their praise in a spectacular way. He delivered them from their jail and misery.

One of the students I had in one of my classes at the seminary had dabbled in the occult early in his life. But then the Lord got hold of him and rescued him from his old life and gave him a new one. He told me that every time he feels harassment from the evil spirit, he sings to the Lord, and the evil spirit leaves. They can't be in the presence of a great and awesome God.

When we sing songs of praise, the spirits don't like it. They have to flee, because they cannot bear to listen.

Martin Luther said, "The devil hates music because he cannot stand gaiety. . . . Satan can smirk but he cannot laugh; he can sneer but cannot sing."[4]

Perhaps that is why we have been told that singing is as much a part of worship as is prayer. The Psalms were often set to music to offer praise to God for what He had done for His people. Let our lives be filled with praise and thanksgiving and songs. When tempted, instead of giving in to our feelings, let us by faith lift up our hearts with songs to God.

We can praise God through musical instruments. The Old Testament is full of references to the playing of musical instruments in praise to God. Those of us who use musical instruments in praise must be careful not to become too dependent upon them so that when the music stops, the praise and worship immediately cease. Our praise should ascend to God even when no instruments are readily available. But God has ordained that musical instruments be used to help facilitate our praises. He created us with musical sensitivities, and He has shown us that the proper response to music should take the form of praise. The Old Testament indicates that musical instruments are more than merely things that we play to accompany worship—they are in and of themselves a praise to God: "Praise him with the sound of the trumpet . . . with the lute and harp . . . with the timbrel and dance . . . with stringed instruments and flutes . . . with loud cymbals . . . with clashing cymbals" (Ps. 150:3-5, NKJV).

Prayer is another way to praise God. It is one of the most effective means of honoring the Lord. Such prayer doesn't have to be public in order to bless Him. Private praise also honors Him. If you wish to express appreciation to some friend of yours, you don't have to arrange for a spot on the evening news or run an ad in the newspaper. You can speak to that individual personally.

The same is true of our praise to God. At times we will want to share it with others through a public statement of thanksgiving for His blessing to us. But perhaps the most personal worship and praise will be in private on our knees.

Although we are the constant recipients of God's mercies, yet how little gratitude we express, how little we praise Him for what He has done for us.

Another way we can praise God is by telling others what He has done for us. Here is one of the reasons Christians should witness. As we share with others God's involvement in our lives, it often arouses their interest. They are drawn to Him as we uplift Him through our praise. The demoniacs who wanted to follow Jesus He told to go back home and relate what great things God had done for them. This avenue for outreach is available to every Christian. You may not be skilled in presenting doctrinal arguments, but you can share with others the experience you have had with Jesus.

THE BENEFITS OF PRAISE

Praise has numerous benefits. It is not just good for God—it's good for us! That's one of the beautiful aspects of God's kingdom. He always arranges to return to us whatever we give to Him—and with dividends! The more we praise Him for His blessings, the more we are blessed.

If we would offer more praise and thanksgiving, we would have far more power in our lives. We would abound more and more in the love of God and have more of His blessings. Should you ever feel that God does not hear your prayers, mingle praise with your petitions. When you consider His goodness and mercies, you will find that He has blessed you greatly.

PERSONAL APPEAL

"Whoever offers praise glorifies Me" (Ps. 50:23, NKJV). So praise the Lord! Praise Him for who He is, for His love and mercy and kindness. Praise Him for what He has done in the past. Praise Him for what He is doing for you today. And praise Him for the promise of what He is going to do in the future. We can praise Him not only in words but by consecrating to Him all that we are and have.

Would you like to offer to God the greatest praise possible? Then become consecrated channels through whom He can work. No matter when, where, or how we praise the Lord, we are to do so with our entire beings. "Bless the Lord, O my soul: and all that is within me, bless his holy name" (Ps. 103:1). In Mark 12:30 Jesus highlighted for us the foremost commandment of all: "Love the Lord your God with all your heart, with all your soul, with all your mind, and with all your strength" (NKJV). This is the pinnacle of praise: to love and praise Him with everything that is within us.

One of the churches I pastored had a member who was nearly blind and deaf, but he never missed a worship service. So one day I said to him, "George, why do you come to church? You can't hear anything. You can't see anything."

Very enthusiastically he replied, "I don't need to see or hear to come to church. I come to church to praise the Lord and serve Him and to tell the whole universe what side I am on. I don't need to hear and see to praise the Lord. My heart is full of the things of God, and they spill over in praise and adoration and thanksgiving." George was right. What we need is not a tongue to praise the Lord, although that is very helpful. What we require is a heart fully engaged with the heart of God.

---

[1] Bob Sorge, *Exploring Worship* (Canandaigua, N.Y.: Bob Sorge, 1987), pp. 1-27.

[2] A. W. Tozer, *Worship: The Missing Jewel of the Evangelical Church* (Harrisburg, Pa.: Christian Publications, 1961), pp. 7, 8.

[3] Sorge, p. 12.

[4] Sammy Tippit, *Worthy of Worship* (Chicago: Moody Press, 1989), p. 90.

*"Through Jesus, therefore, let us continually offer to God a sacrifice of praise—
the fruit of lips that confess his name. And do not forget to do good and to share
with others, for with such sacrifices God is pleased. Obey your leaders and
submit to their authority. They keep watch over you as men who must give an
account. Obey them so that their work will be a joy, not a burden, for that
would be of no advantage to you"* (Heb. 13:15-17, NIV).

8

Offering and Worship

When John Wesley preached his great sermon on stewardship, his first division he titled "Make all you can." A deacon farmer down in the front pew said, "That is right." The second division Wesley labeled "Save all you can," and the farmer said more emphatically, "That is better." And the third division of the sermon was "Give all you can," and the farmer's face dropped. "That has spoiled the sermon," he declared. Now, that farmer had a vision of stewardship in making and in saving, and that is scriptural; but he had lost the vision (if he ever had it) of giving.

In this chapter we consider another vital element of worship: offering. We are not going to speak about money but about worship. Instead of budgets and church needs, we will explore Lordship, allegiance, and trust.

From the very beginning, worshipping God meant bringing an offering to Him. Looking at worship in the Old Testament, we see that in the first recorded act of worship by Cain and Abel, each of them brought an offering to the Lord. It is significant that Abel's offering involved a sacrifice offered by faith while Cain's consisted of an offering of the fruit of the ground. It is, therefore, important to note that the worship of God began with offering.

Throughout the history of Israel God's people erected altars and made offerings upon them to the true God. Whether it was during the lives of the great patriarchs, or in front of the tabernacle in the wilderness, or within the courts of the Temple at Jerusalem, to worship God was to bring an offering to Him. The psalmist gave the invitation clearly: "Give to the Lord the glory due His name; bring an offering, and come into His courts" (Ps. 96:8, NKJV). Here is perhaps the simplest statement in Scriptures as to what worshipping God involves. We should not regard worship chiefly as what we get from God. Rather, worship is giving—it is offering. If there is anything that we need to understand today, it is this fact.

The great majority of the offerings of the Old Testament were sacrifices. Since Jesus Christ offered Himself as the perfect sacrifice for our sins, there no longer exists any need for blood sacrifices. However, because the sacrifice of Christ is the basis of all Christian faith and hope, that sacrifice must, if we are to be faithful to Him, always be prominent in our worship. Christ's sacrifice involves not only His death on Calvary but also His resurrection from the dead and His ascension into heaven itself with the blood of the eternal covenant, as well as His present intercession for the believer (see Heb. 13:20, 21). All this is included in His offering of Himself for sinners. Nothing can ever be added to that sacrifice—it is sufficient for our salvation.

It is clear, nevertheless, that Christians are to continue to sacrifice to the Lord as a part of their worship. One of the most vital doctrines of the New Testament is the priesthood of all believers. The apostle Peter said: "Coming to Him as to a living stone, rejected indeed by men, but chosen by God and precious, you also, as living stones, are being built up a spiritual house, a holy priesthood, to offer up spiritual sacrifices acceptable to God through Jesus Christ" (1 Peter 2:4, 5,

NKJV). Here it is evident that those who belong to the Christian priesthood are to exercise that responsibility by offering up spiritual sacrifices. But they in no sense replace or increase the efficacy of the one offering of Christ. Rather, they are made possible by that one eternal sacrifice and are to be offered as a response to and in perfect union with that ultimate sacrifice.

What are the spiritual sacrifices the apostle Peter tells us that believers should offer to God? Let us look at what the Scriptures explain about them in Hebrews 13:15-17.

We Are to Offer the Lord Our Praises

First, the writer of the Epistle to the Hebrews tells us that we are to present the sacrifice of praise. "Therefore by Him let us continually offer the sacrifice of praise to God, that is, the fruit of our lips, giving thanks to His name" (Heb. 13:15, NKJV). It does not mean that the mere singing of songs or the recitation of prayers with our lips in the worship service constitutes acceptable sacrifice. The "fruit of the lips" must be the response of the heart to the incomprehensible grace of God in Jesus Christ. As we sing and praise God, let us remember that we are to sing our songs to the Lord—to His glory and to His honor—even though they also serve to edify and admonish other believers as well as ourselves. "Let the word of Christ dwell in you richly in all wisdom, teaching and admonishing one another in psalms and hymns and spiritual songs, singing with grace in your hearts to the Lord" (Col. 3:16, NKJV). This is our spiritual sacrifice.

While driving to a meeting last winter, I felt as lifeless as the white sky and frozen roadway stretching before me. *Where was joy?* I wondered. *When would I sing again?* Right away God gave me fresh perspective. Looking up, I noticed telephone wires suspended horizontally across the highway like musical chords. Birds at various levels punctuated the lines like little white notes. As I sped by, insulated by my car's closed window, I couldn't hear them, but I knew they were singing. Reassured, I remembered the psalmist's words: "Sing to the Lord a new song" (Ps. 96:1, NKJV), and I knew that God gave me a song too. Praise and singing provides you new prospective on life, offering you power to face life's challenges.

Peter Buehler, who helped lead John and Charles Wesley to experience conversion, once said, "If I had a thousand tongues, I'd praise Christ with them all." Charles Wesley expanded his stray comment into lines that became the well-known hymn "O for a Thousand Tongues to Sing."

WE ARE TO OFFER THE LORD OUR GOOD WORK

A second spiritual sacrifice that Scripture urges the Christian to give is the doing of good works. "But do not forget to do good and to share, for with such sacrifices God is well pleased" (Heb. 13:16, NKJV). Not all of humanity's good deeds are acceptable to God. Individuals who presume to offer to God their own good deeds instead of placing their full trust and confidence in the sacrifice of Christ are offering a mockery to God. The apostle Paul spoke of the sad condition of those, who in "seeking to establish their own righteousness, have not submitted to the righteousness of God" (Rom. 10:3). He warned such people that "wrath has come upon them" (1 Thess. 2:16, NKJV).

However, the same apostle reminded true believers that they were to "be careful to maintain good works" (Titus 3:8, NKJV). These are the works that comprise a spiritual sacrifice. What do they include? Any deed done because of love for God and the desire to honor Him is a spiritual sacrifice acceptable to God.

The first priority of God's people is to build His kingdom, to serve Him, to pursue His purpose, to glorify His name, and to honor Him in everything they do. They do such things by offering Him their good work.

The focus of all faithful Christians is their Master. Their goal is to bring glory to Him through acts of mercy, love without boundaries, and giving without limits.

Often I hear people say, "But I do not have talent to serve the Lord. I can't sing. I can't preach or witness. And I don't have money to give." It's not the gift that we have that is important, but how we allow God to use it for His glory.

One of the *Ripley's Believe It or Not* strips pictured a plain bar of iron costing $5. The same bar of iron if made into horseshoes would be worth $50. If fashioned into needles, its value would be $5,000. But if transformed into balance springs for fine Swiss watches, the same amount of metal would fetch $500,000. The raw material is not as important as how it's developed. God says that we have spiritual gifts, but their worth to Him will depend on how we cultivate them.[1]

As believers in Jesus Christ, we need to offer our good works to Him—our talents, kindness, love, and even our lives.

WE ARE TO OFFER THE LORD OUR POSSESSIONS

The third spiritual sacrifice mentioned in Hebrews is sharing (Heb. 13:16). Whenever the believer, in sheer thanksgiving to God, shares his or her material substance with those in need or with those engaged in the ministry of the Word, or when he or she cheerfully places a generous check in the offering plate to support the work of God and His church, that person is making an acceptable offering to the Lord.

The receiving of an offering in the worship service should never be looked upon as a necessary interruption of the service, required for the maintenance of the church. It is an important part of worship. Worship is not exclusively offering, but the sincere offering of our possessions and money to God is worship. During the service the presentation of the offering should be impressive, making it clearly evident that it is a response of the entire congregation to God's goodness.

Abraham demonstrated his worship in the tangible act of returning his tithe to God. This simple yet significant act of worship was a public acknowledgment of God's sovereign claim and ownership, as well as His Lordship. The patriarch thus expressed love and gratitude in worship in a tangible way to the God who had blessed him in the fullness of life, prosperity, strength, and hope.

The English Bible has 31,173 verses. About 500 of them are on faith, 500 on prayer, 1,000 on love, and 700 on peace. But 2,400 verses deal with the topic of money and money management. That amounts to more than 7.5 percent of all the verses in the Bible. Fifteen percent of Jesus' words and 23 of the 40 parables of Jesus involve money. Why so much emphasis on the topic? Because, as Larry Burkett said, "money is an outside indicator of an inside spiritual condition."

Jesus Christ said more about money than about any other single thing, because when it comes to a person's real nature, money is of first importance. It is an exact index to an individual's true character. All through Scripture we find an intimate correlation between the development of character and how one handles money.

TITHES AND OFFERINGS ARE SIGNS OF OUR ALLEGIANCE TO GOD

The offering is not a means of paying church bills, but a way to worship God and show allegiance to Him. When you write the check for the church offering, gather the family together and pray over it to help bring out the spiritual significance.

I visited the University of Chicago's Oriental Institute museum a few years ago. Going through the various sections, I noticed that tithing was a common practice in ancient times. It was a sign of lordship and allegiance.

Abraham demonstrated his worship through returning his tithe to God. This simple yet significant act of worship served as a public acknowledgment of God's sovereign claim and ownership as well as His Lordship. It allows human beings to portray love and gratitude in worship in a tangible way.

TITHES AND OFFERINGS ARE ASSOCIATED WITH GOD'S BLESSING

Of all the promises in the Bible, none are more specific than the passages regarding giving. "So let each one give as he purposes in his heart," Paul says, "not grudgingly or of necessity; for God loves a cheerful giver" (2 Cor. 9:7, NKJV). When we give gladly, willingly, or cheerfully, we demonstrate an unselfish attitude of appreciation for what God has done for us by endowing us with new life and hope through Jesus Christ. To be loved by God brings us inner security, joy, and peace of mind.

In spite of the promised blessings and periodic teaching on giving, most Christians fail to return to God what rightfully belongs to Him. Lack of giving could be the result of biblical ignorance on our part, but most likely it reflects a lack of obedience to the admonitions in Scripture. Perhaps it indicates selfishness on our part and unwillingness to share what we possess. Someone has said, "Jesus Christ must be Lord of all or not Lord at all—including, of course, our purse or wallet."

Givers fall into three types: the flint, the sponge, and the honeycomb. Some givers are like a piece of flint—to get anything out of it you must hammer it, and even then you get only chips and sparks. No matter what the need is, or the appeal in church, nothing comes out of them. Others are like a sponge—to get anything out of a sponge, you must squeeze it hard, because the more you squeeze a sponge, the more you get. Therefore, the more skilled the one who asks for the offering, or the more guilt woven into the appeal, the more money obtained. But others are like a honeycomb. Having experienced God's blessing and acceptance and love, they overflow with generosity, love, giving, and sweetness. That is how God gives to us, and it is how we should give in turn. When we give in that kind of spirit, we are indeed worshipping God.

TITHES AND OFFERINGS REVEAL THE PRIORITIES OF OUR LIVES

In Matthew Jesus said, "Do not lay up for yourselves treasures on earth, where moth and rust destroy and where thieves break in and steal; but lay up for yourselves treasures in heaven, where neither moth nor rust destroys and where thieves do not break in and steal. For where your treasure is, there your heart will be also" (Matt. 6:19-21, NKJV).

"I have had my home broken into twice, and I can identify with this passage," Charles Riggs wrote. "We did not have a lot of goods that thieves can market easily; therefore, our loss was minimal. But the experience has given my wife and me a better perspective on life and personal possessions. Our real home is in heaven, not here on earth."[2]

That is the lesson Jesus teaches in this passage. He is not against savings accounts but rather our getting preoccupied with money and things: "Where your treasure is, there will your heart be also" (verse 21). Greed can cause us to be so focused on secular pursuits that we forget why we are here. We are to "lay up treasures in heaven." The more we give to God of our money and service, the more treasure we store up in heaven. But God also offers great dividends here in this life.

Billy Graham once said, "Tell me what you think about money, and I can tell you what you think about God, for these two are closely related. A man's heart is closer to his wallet than almost anything else."[3]

TITHES AND OFFERINGS INDICATE OUR LEVEL OF TRUST IN GOD

God has a purpose in everything that He asks us to do. The tithe is important to the one who gives it—as an obedient response to His command, as an event in our lives that frees us from self-centeredness, as a means to develop our level of trust, and as an opportunity for God to bless us in return.

One day one of the members of a church that I pastored confided in me about his trouble with the concept of tithing and giving. He revealed his doubts to me by saying, "Pastor, I just don't see how I can give 10 percent of my income to the church when I can't even keep on top of my bills."

"Tim," I told him, "if I promise to make up the difference in your bills if you should fall short, do you think you could try tithing for just one month?"

After a moment thinking about it, he replied, "Sure, if you promise to make up any shortage, I guess I could try tithing for one month."

"Now, what do you think of that," I said. "You say you'd be willing to put your trust in a mere man like yourself, who possesses little materially, but you couldn't trust your heavenly Father, who owns the whole universe!" The next Sabbath Tim gave his tithe, and has been doing so faithfully ever since.

I love the story of the young lad in Africa who trusted in God so strongly that he tithed even before he got his fish. One day after going fishing he knocked on the door of the hut occupied by the missionary. When the missionary opened the door, he found the boy holding a large fish in his hands. The boy said, "Pastor, you taught us what tithing is, so here—I've brought you my tithe." As the missionary gratefully took the fish, he questioned the young lad. "If this is your tithe, where are the other nine fish?" At this the boy beamed and said, "Oh, they're still back in the river. I'm going back to catch them."[4]

WE ARE TO OFFER THE LORD OUR LIVES

Finally, God calls all true Christians to offer their bodies continually to the Lord for the living of pure and holy lives before Him. "I beseech you therefore, brethren, by the mercies of God, that you present your bodies a living sacrifice, holy, acceptable to God, which is your reasonable service" (Rom. 12:1, NKJV). In offering our bodies as living sacrifices we unite ourselves with Jesus Christ "who through the eternal Spirit offered Himself without spot to God" (Heb. 9:14, NKJV).

At some point in every worship experience we should make this same climactic dedication of our entire lives to God. Included in such an offering is the willingness to do His will no matter what the cost, to love others with pure Christian love, and to seek in all aspects of life to demonstrate the reality of the living Christ dwelling within. No sacrifice that human beings can offer to God can be a substitute for self-sacrificing and self-offering.

The purpose of life is not marriage, success, happiness, accumulation of money, or any of that. Rather, we live to glorify God. He created us to know and worship Him. Paul says that so elegantly: "Therefore, whether you eat or drink, or whatever you do, do all to the glory of God" (1 Cor. 10:31, NKJV).

In Exodus 29 we read some interesting instructions regarding the worship practices of the Israelites. "And you shall burn the whole ram on the altar. It is a burnt offering to the Lord; it is a sweet aroma, an offering made by fire to the Lord" (verse 18, NKJV).

In the same chapter we encounter several other types of offerings, and the instructions are the same (see verses 7, 8, 25, 30-33, 41, 42).

The primary significance of the sacrificial system of the Old Testament was that it predicted the redemptive work that Jesus would accomplish at Calvary. But the burnt offerings also have a secondary significance. God was not just concerned about the animal that the Israelites slew and sacrificed. Also important to Him was the fragrance, the soothing aroma. God wanted it to be drifting upward continually, perpetually, all the time, throughout all generations—as a symbol of worship. It was as if He were saying, "It is My desire that there be an unending flow of worship ascending heavenward. Each time you walk by the doorway of the tent of meeting, you will see the smoke rising from the altar and remember that you ought to be living in a perpetual state of worship. From your heart there ought to emerge a fragrant aroma of worship ascending to heaven at all times."

The smoke and the aroma were sensory aids that God used to impress upon the Israelites the importance of continual worship. Day and night it served as a symbol of adoration and worship.

What does this insight mean for those of us who desire to be true worshippers of the living God? It suggests that we have to make worship a continual part of our existence—a moment-by-moment gift to God.

A PERSONAL APPEAL

We find an excellent model of true worship (that involves the offering of our praise, good works, possessions, and lives) in the experience of the Magi. Worship is something they came a long way to do. We learn in Matthew 2:16 that Jesus may have been 2 years old by the time the Wise Men showed up. That suggests that they may have been traveling for two years. Thus they must have considered the worship of Jesus a high priority if they spent two years of their lives, time, and possessions to visit the newborn King and worship Him.

Gift-giving also accompanied their worship. It is worth noting that their gifts were substantial ones. The Wise Men didn't run out to Kmart and get a blanket or something on sale. They brought expensive presents, and their gifts were part of their worship, a fact also illustrated in their act of bowing down to symbolize their worship to the newborn King.

The Magi gave of their time as well as their possession, their lives as well as their obedience and worship.

In 1815 Napoleon went down to defeat at the Battle of Waterloo, and the hero of that encounter was the duke of Wellington. The duke's most recent biographer claims to have an advantage over all the other previous ones. He had found an old account ledger that showed how the duke had spent his money. That, says the biographer, was a far better clue to what the man thought was really important than reading his letters or his speeches. What if someone wrote your biography on the basis of your checkbook or your income-tax return, or your work, or your time—what might it say about you, your loyalties, your focus, and about whom you serve?

----

[1] James S. Hewett, *Illustrations Unlimited* (Wheaton, Ill.: Tyndale House Pub., 1988), p. 232.

[2] Charles Riggs, *Learning to Walk With God* (Minneapolis: World Wide Publications, 1988), pp. 158, 159.

[3] In Riggs, p. 154.

[4] See Riggs, p. 458.

"They devoted themselves to the apostles' teaching and to the fellowship, to the breaking of bread and to prayer. Everyone was filled with awe, and many wonders and miraculous signs were done by the apostles. All the believers were together and had everything in common. Selling their possessions and goods, they gave to anyone as he had need. Every day they continued to meet together in the temple courts. They broke bread in their homes and ate together with glad and sincere hearts, praising God and enjoying the favor of all the people. And the Lord added to their number daily those who were being saved" (Acts 2:42-47, NIV).

"We proclaim to you what we have seen and heard, so that you also may have fellowship with us. And our fellowship is with the Father and with his Son, Jesus Christ. We write this to make our joy complete" (1 John 1:3, 4, NIV).

9

The Church of My Dreams

I HAVE ALWAYS BEEN A DREAMER

At 10 years of age I dreamed of gold and of finding great treasure. I read stories of deep-sea diving and how such treasures waited somewhere underneath the sea. My books told of pirates who had stolen millions in gold and, because of shipwrecks and battles at sea, a lot of that gold had sunk into the ocean. Believing that it was still there, I dreamed of it and other hidden treasure.

At age 15 I dreamed of becoming a writer and being on the bestseller list. Although I did some writing, I never made it to the New York *Times* best-seller list. But I made it to my mom's best-reading list. She was nice to me.

Later I dreamed of being a scientist and having my own lab. In fact, I actually began to gather materials to build my own spaceship. I got some boards, boxes, aluminum materials, old fan blades, and nuts and bolts, and was going to construct the spaceship. I dreamed of flying it into outer space and conducting a lot of scientific studies.

By age 20 I decided that I was going to be an engineer. I started to read about designs and ways to develop my spaceship. I decided I was going to be the engineer of the year, design a spaceship, fly it high into outer space, and conduct my scientific studies.

At 25 years of age I dreamed of love and marriage and home and children.

But one day Christ came and called me into another job, and all my dreams have changed. He summoned me to be a minister, and all my dreams started to center on the churches I pastored or belonged to. Often I would sit quietly or lie down at night and dream. Oh, if only all those dreams could come true concerning the church. The world would look at this church and say, "There is the greatest church on earth. There is where God's name is glorified."

Today I dream of a church in which people are passionate about God, totally led by the Spirit, and filled with joy. I dream about a church in which worship is inspiring and praise is contagious. I dream about a church whose members are fully devoted to prayer and the experience of the presence of God. I dream of a group of people excited about the Word of God and fully committed to Him. I dream about believers who are fully devoted followers of Christ and filled with His love, grace, and acceptance. I want to belong to a church like that. I want to belong to a fellowship in which people love me and accept me no matter where I come from, what I say, or even how I behave. It is my dream—my vision.

Churches do not consist of wood and stone. Even though such materials are necessary, they make a building only. Rather, churches consist of men, women, boys, and girls who love God more than life, and honor each other as Jesus loves them. I see my dream church as a group of people filled with love and hope because God is in them and He leads and directs them.

This is my dream church. It is where I want to be—where I want to belong.

THE TIES THAT BIND US

In Acts 2 we find the description of a dream church. It is of a community of faith totally devoted to Jesus. They immerse themselves in the study of Scripture, prayer, and fellowship. Their love for each other leads them to the point of selling their possessions and sharing everything. Miracles and wonderful things characterize their experience. As they worship and praise God, the Lord adds to their number daily. What a dream church—one filled with love, grace, and acceptance. But what makes such a church possible? After all, during the last day of the life of Christ we find His followers denying Him, abandoning Him, and running away from Him. But then the Holy Spirit came upon them, and everything changed. The Holy Spirit turned them inside out, changing them from selfishness to servanthood. Here is what I see as the heart of this church.

No one told this church to be a worshipping community or its members to sell their possessions and give to the poor. They did those things because they loved God.

Nor did anyone order the early church to form a community. I can't imagine the disciples gathering on Pentecost evening trying to figure out what to do with 3,000 people. Can you see Peter suggesting, "Let's have everyone meet together on Sabbath mornings, and we will organize fellowship home groups for midweek. Andrew and Nathanael, find us the natural leaders out of this group and take them on a leadership retreat this weekend. They will head the small groups for us. Thomas, draw up some guidelines for participation, and we will have people sign them. We will require attendance and that the rich sell their property to help the poor . . ."

Absurd, isn't it? Without anyone even thinking of organization, the church became a caring community that worshipped and grew together. The people shared resources so well that no needy existed among them. Even the people around them marveled at the love they had for each other, and many ended up joining the church (see Acts 2:42-47).

Though the model that we see in the New Testament church as a community of faith may be rare today, it is what our hearts desire. What culture, busyness, lack of time, and institutional priorities have destroyed, spiritually hungry people caught up in the wonder of the Savior can regain. As they love Him more than life and worship Him with all their being they naturally desire to be with each other.

If the church is to become the community of God's people and the hope of the world, it demands much more than singing the same hymns, praying the same prayers, partaking of the same Lord's Supper, and joining in the same rituals. It will involve the full commitment of our lives and of all that we have to one another. It is only as we lose our lives that we find them and thus bring the life of Jesus to others.

Why is it so hard for the church today to recapture what came so naturally to the early church? Maybe it is because we are busy, or because we lack commitment, or we do not know how. Or it may simply be that they knew they needed it and we don't think we do. Community rises out of the convergence of two different streams. Identifying them in the early church can help us rediscover them today.

1. THEIR LOVE AND DEVOTION FOR GOD

The church started with only a few thousand people, all of whom were overwhelmed by a fresh revelation and experience of the reality and love and power of God. I have often thought how the life of the fellowship that I attend would differ if we could all capture our own first love on the same day. The joy would be infectious, and so would be our hunger to learn the ways of God.

That joy and hunger are the foundation of community. Without it, everything else is merely an exercise in human relations and will not rise to the splendor of biblical community. Jesus prayed that all His followers would find unity together, but even His prayer makes it clear that there is only one road to unity: "I have given them the glory that you gave me, that they may be one as we are one" (John 17:22, NIV). We are united together when we are united in Christ.

The unity that marks Christian community cannot rise out of tolerance, compromise, or concession. It emerges only among people bonded by their love for God and their intense worship of and devotion to Him. They are fellow worshippers who are seeking to be changed into His image. As God transforms me, I find tremendous compatibility with others who are also changing. Without even trying, I'm suddenly aware of their needs and of how I can help, and I'm also conscious of the insight they can add to my own life.

Community is the result of intimacy, nurtured by an environment of grace, love, and mutual understanding. Scripture links our spiritual health to community involvement with other believers. Only believers who can speak the truth in love with each other "will in all things grow up into him who is the Head" (Eph. 4:15, NIV); and only by being "encouraged in heart and united in love" can we "have the full riches of complete understanding" (Col. 2:2, NIV).

For people hungering after God, opening their lives to others is not a cumbersome obedience but a valuable resource of encouragement, strength, and hope.

We need to have a fresh experience of the reality and love of God daily as we constantly seek to recapture our first love for Jesus and His purpose. Such encounters with the Spirit will fill our being with God's grace and acceptance. Without that deep and lasting fellowship with Him, our communion with each other is again nothing but human relations. Jesus prayed for us to be united much the same as the union that He has with the Father.

"I have given them the glory that you gave me, that they may be one as we are one: I in them and you in me. May they be brought to complete unity to let the world know that you sent me and have loved them even as you have loved me. Father, I want those you have given me to be with me where I am, and to see my glory, the glory you have given me because you loved me before the creation of the world. Righteous Father, though the world does not know you, I know you, and they know that you have sent me. I have made you known to them, and will continue to make you known in order that the love you have for me may be in them and that I myself may be in them" (John 17:22-26, NIV).

I find fellowship with people who seek to grow into Christ's likeness to be especially irresistible and meaningful. As this takes place, we discover that our health and growth are linked to our involvement with the community.

The early believers had common hope, faith, love, struggle, goals, and destiny. It was the basis of their fellowship, and it should be that of ours.

2. THE REALITY OF THEIR STRUGGLE

Imagine yourself awakening on a forest floor, your head racked with pain. For a moment you can't remember where you are or why you hurt so badly. Looking around in the increasing light of early dawn, you note the wispy columns of smoke rising from the twisted wreckage of an aircraft. You see the clearing carved out by the plane's descent and crash. Then you remember the exploding antiaircraft shells in the pitch-black sky around you, a violent jolt, and a sharp left descending turn. The plane's pitch was too steep to bail out until just over the trees.

Moans of pain call you back to the present. There are other survivors—10 to be exact, all with injuries and without any medical supplies. Since you are 200 miles inside enemy lines, the only rescue party you can expect will make you prisoners of war.

Now, such individuals aren't going to fight for position or waste time complaining about their circumstances. Instead, they will channel all their energies into continuing with their mission, if possible, and if not, then into creating havoc for the enemy while they try to get back across the enemy lines. They will mold each person's gifts and abilities into a great team that stands the best possible chance of achieving their goal.

The early church understood the desperate reality of their circumstances, and their cooperation with each other matched that perception. Jesus had warned them how fragile life was in a world hostile toward God and dominated by an enemy bent on their destruction. They shared and ministered without the petty political concerns that normally drain church life. Recognizing that they were in occupied country, they endeavored to please God even when they knew that so much in them wanted to please themselves.

No one told them they needed each other—they just knew it. Circumstances haven't changed—only our perception of them. We are still at war. Casualties line our streets and the enemy encircles us with his forces, but we don't see it. The reason that church life today finds itself caught in so many organizational headaches and gets dragged down by the ambitions of others is that it realizes neither the desperateness of its situation nor the fragility of its life. Community is a practical response, not a philosophical one. When you need God desperately, you will find yourself teaming up with others who do too, for the mutual benefit of all.

In high school I was supposed to give a short speech on brotherhood. Simple enough! I assumed that I could dash that off in minutes and have plenty of time for a little television. All of my classmates finished the assignment quickly, but I was stuck. No matter how hard I tried, I could not write a short speech on brotherhood. I thought about brotherhood and fellowship in the context of the Bible. I knew that many of my "friends/brothers" were non-Christians. I did not have much in common with many of them. They were good guys, but they weren't and never could be my brothers in the full sense of that word. I would write a few sentences and then rip that page off and start again. Finally I completed my task, but I knew my paper lacked integrity. I have never forgotten that exercise. I discovered that my bonds to others were based on mutual interest, while those with my brothers and sisters in the Lord derived from our love and commitment to Jesus. Authentic brotherhood and fellowship are found only in Christ.

My Dream Church

Let me tell you about the characteristics of my dream church.

1. A LOVING CHURCH

My dream church is a loving church.

The New Testament is a place in which we can find community, healing, and love. We can belong to lots of things, but I see the church of Jesus Christ as an extended family, something beyond that of any other kind of group.

I remember my boy, when he was small, running full speed through the sanctuary of the church. My good friend, Phil, reached out and grabbed him by the collar. The child's little legs were still going, and Phil was holding him there. "Jason, slow down!" Phil said.

Jason looked at him and protested, "Put me down! You're not my dad."

"No, I'm not your dad, but I'm your uncle," my friend replied. "I'm your uncle because your daddy is my brother in Christ, and I love you as much as if you were my real nephew. I want to help you become the kind of man you ought to be. So you just slow down. OK?" We need that in a church—to care for each other's sons and daughters.

When people's lives come unglued and the effects of culture absolutely

93

destroy them, where can they go to find forgiveness and understanding? To a group that will accept them in a nonjudgmental fashion and simply say, "We love you. We'll help you." I believe in the church of Jesus Christ, because it's a place I can find community, healing, and love.

I believe in the church because it has provided motivation for the most loving, lasting, valuable, and selfless efforts of humanity. It has inspired such things as schools, hospitals, orphanages, relief agencies, the abolition of slavery, the promotion of women's rights, and the end of child labor. Such institutions and movement came into being when men and women, moved by God against the backdrop of His holy justice, decided to change the world.

If you were to remove the influence of Christian missions from the world today, it would implode from its lack of morality.

Some of you may have read Barbara Tuckman's great historical account *The Distant Mirror,* in which she records that during one period of the Middle Ages, one third of the population of the entire earth from Moscow to Cairo died of the Black Plague. Who were those men in brown outfits out picking up the dead and caring for the sick? Christians went out in the name of Jesus Christ to alleviate the greatest suffering our world had yet seen.

If we produced a schematic drawing of the church, it would be far more complicated than that of some device such as a television or a computer. It would involve every one of our lives. But when you finish looking at that schematic, it wouldn't be a bunch of arrows aimed at a central point so that we could come together and sing, "Hold the fort, for I am coming." Rather, it would be a great group of arrows flying outward as a man opens a business, a woman starts teaching, another woman goes into homemaking, a man works as a plumber, someone enrolls as a student, and still another person serves as a nurse. We all go out into the world to be the church of Jesus Christ. Aren't you glad to be part of something that is world-changing, that has stood for 2,000 years, that makes a difference?

A story called "The Rabbi's Gift" has profoundly influenced me.

It is the story of a dying monastery at the edge of a beautiful forest. Once it had been a thriving community filled with people who had served the Lord in a variety of ways, but its membership had dwindled through the years, until finally only five brothers remained. All were elderly and lonely.

Sometimes a wise rabbi went out into the nearby forest to meditate by himself. The abbot of the monastery and the Jewish rabbi were good friends, and often they talked. Many times the abbot would explain that things were not going well at the monastery and comment that he didn't think it would last much longer. Did the Jewish leader have any suggestions as to how the abbot could halt what seemed to be the monastery's inevitable fate?

"I have no wisdom for you," the rabbi said sadly, shaking his head. "I'm sorry."

They would read the Scriptures together, and weep together for a while; then each would return home.

But one day the rabbi said, "I don't know why, but I do have a word for you today." It wasn't really a word of advice, nor did it have anything to do with the troubles of the monastery. The rabbi said to the abbot, "The Messiah is one of you." Then both of them shook their heads and thought, *That's strange.*

After they finished their usual Scripture reading and their prayers, the abbot returned to the monastery. As always at mealtime his comrades asked him, "What did you talk about today?"

"It was interesting," the abbot began. "The rabbi said, 'The Messiah is one of you.'" For a moment they all chuckled, and no one mentioned it again.

But during the following months something changed in that monastery—something subtle yet warm and fresh and new. Each of the brothers began to think about that statement "The Messiah is one of you," and began to study the others closely. Gradually they began to see little ways in which that statement might be true about someone else. Maybe the abbot was, indeed, the Messiah. Perhaps Brother Philip was. Or could it be Brother Thomas or Brother Aelred or—certainly, each of them had some of the graces that would be a characteristic of the Messiah's life.

As time went on they started to treat each other more kindly and became more respectful to each other. They soon sought each other out for fellowship and wisdom. And something began to happen in that community. Love began to blossom in it.

Because of its beauty people had long come from the surrounding villages to have picnic lunches on the monastery grounds. Now more and more people seemed to visit, and they seemed to stay longer and to enjoy talking more with the members of the little community. One day some people asked if they could actually stay in the monastery with the brothers, if they could learn from them what love was about, and if they could share in the rich spirituality they had begun to sense in the place.

The monastery became a haven for the hurting, a family for the lonely, a place of healing for those who had gone through terrible times. One day they decided not to call it a monastery anymore. Instead, they referred to it as a community—Messiah's Community. And over the gates of each entrance they wrote a single line: "The Messiah Welcomes You."

Maybe that's what happened at Corinth. Maybe that's what Paul's letter did as people reflected on seeing Christ in one another, in connecting to the head and the power source of energy. It could have happened there, and it certainly should have, for they were people who were learning to know the mind of Christ. They all felt the same surging of the Spirit within.

But it's not really important what happened in Corinth—whether they became a living example of the body of Christ or not. The one thing that's vital to you and me is the question of what we are and what we together will become in this place.

God is calling us to love each other as He has loved us. He longs for us to love each other as if each one of us is the Messiah.

2. A UNITED CHURCH

In Ephesians 4 Paul urged the believers to walk in a manner worthy of their calling. One aspect of that journey is our diligence in preserving "the unity of the Spirit in the bond of peace" (verse 3, NKJV). Here Paul referred to the church as the body of Christ made up of all believers. Think about it. We who are many are actually one body in Christ. What an amazing realization. You and I are part of the body of Christ.

He Himself is our peace, having made us all into one and broken down the barriers that divide us (see Eph. 2:14). Paul writes: "So then you are no longer strangers and aliens, but you are fellow citizens with the saints, and are of God's household, having been built upon the foundation of the apostles and prophets, Christ Jesus Himself being the corner stone, in whom the whole building, been fitted together, is growing into a holy temple in the Lord, in whom you also are being built together into a dwelling of God in the Spirit" (verses 19-22, NASB).

How does this unity take place? The Holy Spirit is in view here. He alone gives life and unity to the church, even as He inaugurated it on the day of Pentecost. We are all God's creation, and all believers are His children by redemption in Christ. Of necessity, then, we are related to one another because we all have one Father.

But we will not create fellowship by simply setting aside a room in our church for activities that usually center on eating. Nor will we create it through the formation of small groups. Fellowship is, first of all, a common experience of faith—a unique and divine work of the Holy Spirit. It comes only from a true grasp of who we are in Christ.

Such fellowship will never happen unless there develops a wonderful connection with Jesus Christ. Salvation, while we must receive it personally and individually, is never an isolated experience. By our incorporation in Christ we become part of the building that He is constantly constructing (see Matt. 16:18).

Coercion cannot impose community. It must be freely chosen and lived out daily, like everything else about our faith. Many people in recent years have tried to enforce community among believers. Unbiblical methodology supplanted the biblical goal. Community can result only from the Spirit of God stirring people to submit their lives to one another. Nothing can short-circuit this. Believers who have been to the cross together will walk away from it ready to discover the joy of community. The cross is the heart of all fellowship, and it is only through the cross that fellowship deepens and matures. But it requires the frequent and painful crucifixion of self in all its forms—self-seeking, self-centeredness, self-righteousness—and the willingness to remain vulnerable in open fellowship with other Christians. It is a banquet with all present declaring, "I don't deserve to be here, but I am here because of Jesus.

Christ made all of us into one body. Paul underlined this truth with numerous word pictures. The Savior has broken down "the dividing wall" (Eph. 2:14, NASB). He has made "the two into one new man" (verse 15, NASB), has reconciled "them both in one body" (verse 16, NASB), and has "put to death the enmity" (verse 16, NASB). His death on the cross has abolished the sins of the Jews and Gentiles alike (verse 16).

When people are brought near to God through Christ and continue to abide in Him, they find peace with one another. Compromise on either side does not solve divisions, except by peace in Christ. "The way of sal-

97

vation" is singular, and therefore all of us must come together at this point of access to God through the cross. The peace that results through our response to the proclamation of the gospel puts us all on common footing in the presence of God the Father.

3. A SHARING CHURCH

Fellowship is more than what we share in together. It also involves what we share out together. *Koinonia* ("fellowship") in the New Testament concerns not only what we possess but what we do together; not only our common inheritance but also our joint service. Luke uses the word *koinonoi* to describe the business relationship between two pairs of brothers: James and John, Andrew and Simon. They were "partners," he says. C. H. Dodd explains this as meaning that they were "joint owners of the little fishing fleet," but it surely means also that they were colleagues, engaged together in the same fishing trade (see Luke 5:10).★

4. A WORSHIPPING CHURCH

To worship God is to honor Him and give reverence to Him as a divine or supernatural power. To worship God is to regard Him with great or extravagant respect. And to worship is to adore, respect, and esteem God as the source of life and the ruler of the universe.

To worship is to act as an inferior before a superior. When I worship the Lord, I am saying by my actions, "God, You are better than I am. You are bigger than I am. You are more than I am." That was the experience of the early church. God was everything to them.

Such worship manifested itself in praise and thanksgiving. Worship also led them to meet together with joy and simplicity. They were able to say, as did David, "[We were] glad when they said unto [us], Let us go into the house of the Lord" (Ps. 122:1). And worship as well led them to give generously of their time, talents, position, and even lives. They experienced what true worship is all about, which is having God sitting not only on His throne in the center of the universe, but on the throne that stands in the center of their hearts.

A long time ago the Danish philosopher Kierkegaard wrote that most people view worship as a play in which God is the producer, the pastor is the actor, and the congregation are the audience. But in true worship God is the audience, the people are the actors, and the pastor is the prompter. Well, the early church knew what true worship is all about, and they lived it. My prayer is that we do the same under the power and the guidance of the Spirit.

THE HEART OF THE MATTER

How does such a wonderful church happen? When people begin—together—to take their cues from Jesus Christ as the head of the body. When I'm surrounded by other people who are wanting and thinking and doing the same things, I belong—I belong to Christ, and I belong to others because they also belong to Christ. Community becomes a reality not out of our ability to get along, but out of our connection to the same source of thought and power.

Paul tells us even more. True community occurs when the power that drives each of us is the single power of the Holy Spirit. The Holy Spirit of God, he says, is the heartbeat and lifeblood of the community. He is God living within each of us, giving us personal attention, direction, and motivation to be all that we can be. The mind of Christ and the power of the Spirit is what makes community.

I have focused on one simple point in this entire chapter: community can take place only among disciples—people desiring to be changed by Christ into His image. The reason that community is so elusive is because most church meetings are geared to people who want to serve God only nominally.

Personal Experience

MY OWN STORY

I grow up in the biblical city of Nineveh, known today as Mosul, in the northern section of Iraq. My mother and father were wonderful and loving parents. They belonged to the Greek Orthodox Church. Though in many ways they were nominal Christians, my mother showed a lot more commitment to the Lord and the church. But when I accepted Jesus into my heart and became an Adventist, my family turned against me and disowned me. In that part of the world, if you change your religion, it is like renouncing your identity, family, and future, and turning against everything in your culture and heritage.

My family ended up beating me almost to death, then threw me out on the street unconscious. On that day I lost everything—friends, family, and identity. It was the most traumatic time of my life. In the Middle East it is very difficult, if not impossible, to survive without the aid of your family.

When I regained consciousness, I felt the Holy Spirit guiding me to go an Adventist family from the church in Bagdad. Wonderful people, they took me in and ministered to all my needs—physical, emotional, and spiritual. I would not have been able to make it without them. They showed me that although I had lost my birth family, I had found a new family. Though my friends turned against me and persecuted me, God provided new family and friends for me in Christ.

Have you ever thought of the biblical fact that there are more things in common between you and the people who believe in Jesus and devote their lives to serving Him than between you and your physical brothers and sisters?

It is not our physical connection to others that establishes the greatest bonds of fellowship, but rather our devotion and love for Jesus and our reliance on Him that binds and ties us together in an unbroken chain of love and encouragement to each other. I found the fellowship of my brothers and sisters in Jesus to be the source of hope that kept me going.

I love the church. I found in it my new family and friends. I want to be that kind of friend to others.

---

* C. H. Dodd, in George Panikvlam, *Koinōnia in the New Testament* (Rome: Biblical Institute Press, 1979), p. 3.

" 'You are worthy to take the scroll,

And to open its seals;

For You were slain,

And have redeemed us to God by Your blood

Out of every tribe and tongue and people and nation,

And have made us kings and priests to our God;

And we shall reign on the earth.' . . .

'Worthy is the Lamb who was slain

To receive power and riches and wisdom,

And strength and honor and glory and blessing!'"

(Rev. 5:9-12, NKJV).

10

The Thrill of Worship

*T*rue worship involves wonder. Wonder is an overwhelming aware-ness of God's majesty, awesomeness, and greatness. It is adoration born out of a sense of catching a vision of the divine attributes, character, and love. The trouble is that wonder is a rare ingredient. You do not often find it present in most modern worship. After all, what is there to wonder at? We assume that we know all about God, because we listen to sermons and read books that explain what God and the Christian life are all about. After we have outlined the Bible and analyzed God's attributes, what still remains to inspire our wonder?

Furthermore, we live in the space age and have watched rockets and space shuttles take off and return. Human beings have landed and walked on the moon. Thanks to TV, we have seen everything from the conception of a baby to the eruption of a volcano. No more mystery, no more wonder, lingers in our world. Neither the mystery of God, His awesome creative power, nor even His revelation of grace any longer amazes us. We have descriptions and definitions for everything scientific and theological.

If worship is to be meaningful, it must involve wonder, which demands that we learn to accept things that we cannot understand, and appreciate things that we can admire but not explain. Worship is the exercise of the mind and the heart in the contemplation of God in which wonder and awe play an important part in stretching and enlarging our vision of His greatness, grace, and unbelievable love.

The Meaning of Wonder

Many different words encompass the idea of wonder: "amazement," "surprise," "astonishment," "bewilderment," "admiration," "awe," and "fascination," to cite but a few. The word in the Hebrew Bible ("His name will be called Wonderful" [Isa. 9:6, NKJV]) means "to distinguish, to separate." It carries the idea of that which is unique, distinguished, or different. Our English versions translate the word as "hidden," "marvelous," "too high," and "too hard." The Greek words in the New Testament have similar renderings: "amazement," "marvelous," "admiration," "wonderful work."[1] In harmony with such synonyms, we must recognize the fact that true wonder is not a passing emotion or some kind of shallow excitement. It has depth and value to it and enriches the life. Above all, it is an encounter with God that brings awe to the heart. We find ourselves overwhelmed with an emotion that mingles gratitude, adoration, reverence, fear, and love. Instead of looking for explanations, we discover ourselves lost in the immensity and incomprehensibility of God's love.

Rather than being born from ignorance, wonder arises from knowledge. The more that people know about God and His love, the more overwhelmed they are. Scientific or theological *facts* may give some people a big head, but *truths* bring to the reverent worshipping believer a thrilling encounter with God.

Wonder is the seed of spiritual understanding. Moses staring at the burning bush and Peter struggling with the breaking nets illustrate this truth clearly. Both men had their lives changed because they were amazed at something that God did in them. Whether in our private devotions, our daily work, or the corporate worship of the church, we must cultivate an attitude of wonder. We can never tell when we may encounter our own burning bush or breaking net. But when we do behold God, we must exclaim, "Wow, what a God we have—WOW!" And that experience could mark the beginning of the transformation of our being.

God is wonderful in what He is, what He says, and what He does, and such wonder is totally beyond us. "Behold, God is great, and we do not know Him," Elihu said (Job 36:26, NKJV). "Can you search out the deep things of God?" Zophar demanded of Job. "Can you find out the limits of the Almighty?" (Job 11:7, NKJV). Paul asserts: "Oh, the depth of the riches both of the wisdom and knowledge of God! How unsearchable are His judgments and His ways past finding out!" (Rom. 11:33, NKJV).

THE WONDER OF THE CREATOR

Throughout Scripture we find the wonder of God revealed in many ways, but I want to focus on four of the worship hymns recorded in the book of Revelation. What the hosts of heaven are saying and doing in their worship ought to be worthy of our study and imitation. The first hymn, appearing in Revelation 4, emphasizes the wonder of God as Creator.

"Before the throne there was a sea of glass, like crystal. And in the midst of the throne, and around the throne, were four living creatures full of eyes in front and in back. The first living creature was like a lion, the second living creature like a calf, the third living creature had a face like a man, and the fourth living creature was like a flying eagle. The four living creatures, each having six wings, were full of eyes around and within. And they do not rest day or night, saying: 'Holy, Holy, Holy, Lord God Almighty, who was and is and is to come!'

"Whenever the living creatures give glory and honor and thanks to Him who sits on the throne, who lives forever and ever, the twenty-four elders fall down before Him who sits on the throne and worship Him who lives forever and ever, and cast their crowns before the throne, saying: 'You are worthy, O Lord, to receive glory and honor and power; for You created all things, and by Your will they exist and were created'" (verses 6-11, NKJV).

You note, of course, that the theme of their worship is God as the

Creator. David expressed the same attitude centuries ago: "The heavens declare the glory of God; and the firmament shows His handiwork" (Ps. 19:1, NKJV).

What we see in creation pretty much depends on what we have in our hearts. The adoring believer joyfully accepts creation as a window through which we may perceive the Creator. The skeptical, as well as the nominal believer, look at creation and view it not as a window but as a mirror. When we gaze at creation and see reflected only ourselves, then we start to think that we are the Creator, and the result is idolatry.

As you listen to the "creation hymn" recorded in Revelation 4, you discover a great deal about God. He is certainly the sovereign deity, for He is enthroned (the word "throne" appears 14 times in the chapter) and His name is "Lord God Almighty." The Greek text of Revelation uses this name six times and "Almighty" nine times. The only other book in the Bible that employs this name as extensively is that of Job, which certainly emphasizes God in His sovereignty and power.

The heavenly hosts worship a sovereign God who is holy. There is none like Him. He is pure: "God is light" (1 John 1:5, NKJV). Creation is God's holy gift to us, and as its stewards, we must use it for the good of our fellow human beings and to the glory of God. In Revelation 4 we have the 24 elders falling down at God's throne and worshipping the Creator (verses 10, 11). Then in Revelation 5 you will find the same group worshipping the Redeemer (verses 8, 9). Why? Because until human beings acknowledge that they are creatures answerable to a Creator, they can never confess that they are also sinners who need a Redeemer. This explains why Paul, when addressing Gentile audiences, began with God the Creator (Acts 14:5-17). To the Jews Paul stressed God's covenant with Israel, while to the Gentiles he stressed God's covenant with creation. We need this same emphasis today both in our witness and in our worship.

During my early years as a Christian I would argue, "The important thing is the cross!" I did not realize then as I do now that the God of creation and the God of salvation are the same deity, and that we must not divorce Them from each other. I'd like to suggest what it might mean to us to worship an awesome and great God who has created all things. We know, for instance, that we are living in a galaxy that is spinning like a great, oblong pinwheel through time and space. At the point where we're riding on Planet Earth, we're traveling along at approximately 136 miles per second, or 490,000 miles per hour. At this speed we make one rotation in 200 million years. Now, our galaxy is a fairly expansive place. If you want to go across it at its narrowest, and you journey at the speed of light (we know that the speed of light is about 186,000 miles per second—that's moving right along) you can make the trip in 20,000 years. But if you take the longer scenic view, it would require 100,000 years. Our galaxy is about five times as long as it is wide, thus 100,000 years to traverse its length.

Our sun is a relatively minor star—not mediocre, but minor to a degree. It is about 110 times the size of our earth in diameter, or about 860,000 miles in diameter. However, we do have a star in our galaxy—1 Antares—that is large enough that you could put our sun, our moon, and all the planets out to the orbit of Mars inside it.

Astronomers know of the existence of billions of other galaxies like our own. They now tell us that the number of stars in the universe exceeds the number of grains of sand on all the beaches of all the seas of the entire earth.[2]

How does this relate to me? If the God who made the heavens and the earth is my Deity, there is absolutely no problem too big for Him. It's impossible for me to come up with a situation beyond the ability of the God who made the heavens and the earth to solve. I'm serving the Creator God, and He can deal with any difficulty that I might face. The Lord is the alpha and omega, the beginning and the end. He is the Almighty.

What challenge have you been struggling with all week? What has so consumed your mind that you can't even concentrate on your family or your work? Perhaps you're bringing whatever is troubling you to a God who's too small when you need to hand it over to a God who is big enough to handle it.

I often think, *How strange it is that as human beings have expanded their ability to understand the universe, they have lost their ability to grasp the greatness of God.* Another result of our awareness of God as Creator ought to be our faithful stewardship of what He has given us. People who know how to worship the Creator will also know how to use their means in His service. The proper worship of God the Creator could be a step toward solving some of the churches' budget problems. "The earth is the Lord's, and all its fullness" (Ps. 24:1, NKJV). David knew this truth, and that is why he said to the Lord, "For all things come from You, and of Your own we have given You" (1 Chron. 29:14, NKJV). If we all worshiped the Creator as did King David, we would be as generous as he was.

Knowing the Creator is also a great help in practical Christian living. Your adoring response of worship to Him ought to help cure you of worry. At least that is what Jesus taught in the Sermon on the Mount (Matt. 6:19-34). The rich struggle with a constant sense of concern because they do not have enough and struggle to protect what they need. Jesus did not give a lecture on budgets. Instead, He pointed to God's bounty in creation—His care of the birds and flowers—and then made His point: put God first, trust Him, and you will not have to worry.

"Remember now your Creator in the days of your youth," admonished Solomon as he brought the book of Ecclesiastes to a close (Eccl. 12:1, NKJV). Knowing and worshipping the Creator is a sure antidote to pessimism and a cynical approach to life. The believer who sings the praises of the Creator is not likely to go around muttering, "Vanity of vanities, all is vanity" (Eccl. 1:2). Rather, he will join with Paul and shout, "Therefore, my beloved brethren, be steadfast, immovable, always abounding in the work of the Lord, knowing that your labor is not in vain in the Lord" (1 Cor. 15:58, NKJV).

Finally, when we know and worship the Creator, we can face personal suffering and take it and use it for God's glory. "Therefore let those who suffer according to the will of God commit their souls to Him in doing good, as to a faithful Creator" (1 Peter 4:19, NKJV). Not a "faithful King" or even a "faithful Savior," but "a faithful Creator." Only a faithful Creator can make "all things to work together for good to those who love God" (Rom. 8:28, NASB).

THE WONDER OF THE REDEEMER

The wonder of God in creation is but the beginning. We must now consider His awesomeness in redemption.

"'You are worthy to take the scroll,
And open its seals;
For You were slain,
And have redeemed us to God by Your blood

Out of every tribe and tongue and people and nation,
And have made us kings and priests to our God;
And we shall reign on the earth.' . . .
'Worthy is the Lamb who was slain
To receive power and riches and wisdom,
And strength and honor and glory and blessing!' "
(Rev. 5:9-12, NKJV).

Most of us feel very much at home with the theme of redemption, because the cross of Christ is central in our theology and our worship, and rightly so. The atonement is the crucial doctrine of the faith. Unless we are right here it matters little—or so it seems to me—what we are like elsewhere. According to the hosts of heaven, the cross means *redemption.*

It is tragic when a believer loses the wonder of what it means to be redeemed. Christians are those who are constantly amazed at the fact that they are forgiven. They do not take it for granted. One reason we have baptism and the Lord's Supper is that they might remind us of the price that Jesus paid to save us. He has taken the wounds of Calvary to heaven with Him, perhaps to keep before us *forever* that He died in our stead.

Twenty-eight times the book of Revelation refers to Jesus as "the Lamb." The Greek word means "a little pet lamb," the kind that you would not want to see slain for any reason. The major themes of Revelation all allude to the Lamb. God's wrath is "the wrath of the Lamb" (Rev. 6:16). The saints are washed "in the blood of the Lamb" (Rev. 7:14), and the church is "the bride, the Lamb's wife" (Rev. 21:9, NKJV). The heavenly throne is "the throne of God and of the Lamb" (Rev. 22:1, 3, NKJV). Eliminate the Lamb—redemption—from the book of Revelation, and you will have very little left!

We worship the Lamb, and wonder at the Lamb, because of who He is. He is both human and divine, for He is "the Root of David" (Rev. 5:5) as well as the Lamb of God. The phrase alludes to our Lord's human Jewish ancestry (Isa. 11:1, 10). As a result, He has both humanity and sovereignty, for He is "the Lion of the tribe of Judah" (Rev. 5:5, NKJV; see also Gen. 49:8-10). Jesus is both Redeemer and Ruler; Savior and Sovereign. The nature of our Lord, His birth, life and death, is enough to excite the wonder in our hearts! Paul was right: "Without controversy great is the mystery of godliness: God was manifested in the flesh" (1 Tim. 3:16, NKJV).

Consider John's symbolic description of the Lamb: "Having seven horns and seven eyes, which are the seven Spirits of God sent out into all the earth" (Rev. 5:6, NKJV). Seven, of course, is, in the Bible, the number of perfection. Here we have "seven horns" symbolizing perfect power; "seven eyes" symbolizing perfect wisdom; and "seven Spirits" symbolizing His perfect presence in all the earth. The Lamb is omnipotent, omniscient, and omnipresent!

We worship Him because of what He is and because of where He is—at the very throne of heaven. The Father is *on* the throne, and the Lamb is "in the midst of the throne" (verse 6, NKJV). Jesus Christ stands in the center of that series of concentric circles that includes all the hosts of heaven. He is not on earth in a manger or a boat, or even on a cross. Instead, He is in heaven—at the center of heaven's worship! The inhabitants of heaven exalt Him "far above all principality and power and might and dominion, and every name that is named, not only in this age but also in that which is to come" (Eph. 1:21, NKJV).

We worship Him not only for who He is and where He is, but also what He has done for us. His was a sacrificial death for the sins of the whole world, "every tribe and tongue and people and nation" (Rev. 5:9). As we worship the Lamb, we are bearing witness to the good news of the gospel that must be taken to the ends of the earth.

The praise of the heavenly hosts recorded in Revelation 5 contains the elements of a balanced worship. They sang a gospel song about the blood of the Lamb that redeems sinners; they reminded the church of its exalted position as kings and priests; and they even touched on future events: "We shall reign on the earth" (verse 10, NKJV). It is a good model for us to follow if we want our own worship to be balanced.

When I told my young daughter the story of Abraham and Isaac, and how God had finally told Abraham not to kill Isaac and had provided a sacrificial lamb instead, she looked up with a sad expression and said, "I don't like killing lambs." Speechless for a moment, I began to grasp more fully what traumatic and memorable events such sacrifices must have been. The seriousness of killing a lamb for sacrifice overwhelmed me. As never before I realized how horrible sin is and how grace is so amazing. If the killing of a pure white lamb seems horrendous, how immeasurably more was the crucifixion of the Lamb of God.

THE WONDER OF THE KING

Revelation 11:15-18 records the third worship scene. It emphasizes the praising of Christ as the King.

"We give You thanks, O Lord God Almighty,
The One who is and who was and who is to come,
Because You have taken Your great power and reigned.
The nations were angry, and Your wrath has come,
And the time of the dead, that they should be judged,
And that You should reward Your servants the prophets and the saints,
And those who fear Your name, small and great,
And should destroy those who destroy the earth" (verses 17, 18, NKJV).

Here is actually a hymn of thanksgiving, and the participants are praising Jesus Christ for three specific blessings.

First, they praise Him because He reigns supremely. Loud voices in heaven proclaiming "The kingdoms of this world have become the kingdoms of our Lord and of His Christ, and He shall reign forever and ever!" (verse 15, NKJV) trigger the hymn. The King has taken His throne!

Jesus Christ reigns today as our priest-king, seated on the Father's throne (Rev. 3:21). Our Melchizedek, King of Righteousness and King of Peace (Heb. 6:20, 7:1-3), He graciously rules in the lives of willing believers and exercises His authority through His Word and His Spirit. But one day He will have absolute authority when He takes His great power and reigns in an even fuller sense.

While it is not too difficult for us to worship the King of kings and Lord of lords who wore a crown of thorns for us, it is the next blessing that enfolds us. We praise Jesus Christ because He shall judge righteously the wicked and the destroyers of the earth, and will vindicate His followers.

Is it right to praise a God of judgment? If we worship the Lamb that was slain, then we must believe in God's holy judgment on sin. Since God could judge His sinless Son, who became our substitute, why can He not judge sinful nations and rebellious sinners? A sentimental view of the cross leads to a sentimental view of sin, resulting in a condescending God who is complacent toward sin and tolerant of sinners. But this is not the God who elicits the praises of the hosts of heaven!

Most of the songs about future events emphasize the more positive doctrines: the redemption of humanity, the reunion of God's people, and the restoration of everlasting life. But why praise the Lord because He is coming to judge? Because that is what the hosts of heaven do! In fact, all of nature anticipates the arrival of the divine Judge and the deliverance He brings us from the bondage of sin.

> "Let the heavens rejoice, and let the earth be glad;
> Let the sea roar, and all it fullness;
> Let the field be joyful, and all that is in it.
> Then all the trees of the woods will rejoice before the Lord.
> For He is coming, for He is coming to judge the earth.
> He shall judge the world with righteousness,
> And the peoples with His truth" (Ps. 96:11-13, NKJV).

If we find ourselves unmoved by the wonder of God's judgment, then either we have forgotten what sin is really like, or we have lost our vision of the holiness of God. It is not enough to preach, "God is love." We must also declare: "For our God is a consuming fire" (Heb. 12:29, NKJV). God is calling us to live a holy and righteous life, full of obedience and love. The holiness of God is a source of inspiration and motivation to live the way that He does.

The third blessing that summons forth the praises of the heavenly hosts is the fact that Christ righteously rewards His servants. They all have in common the fact that they fear His name; they stand in awe of God and His holy name; and by their faithful lives and service, they seek to honor that name.

THE WONDER OF THE BRIDEGROOM

The fourth worship scene focuses on the conquering Bridegroom and presents the great "Heavenly Hallelujah Chorus."

"After these things I heard a loud voice of a great multitude in heaven, saying, 'Alleluia! Salvation and glory and honor and power belong to the Lord our God! For true and righteous are His judgments, because He has judged the great harlot who corrupted the earth with her fornication; and He has avenged on her the blood of His servants shed by her.' Again they said, 'Alleluia! Her smoke rises up forever and ever!'" (Rev. 19:1-3, NKJV).

Unable to remain silent, the elders respond with "Amen! Alleluia!" And then a great multitude climaxes this heavenly "Hallelujah Chorus" with: "Alleluia! For the Lord God Omnipotent reigns!" (verse 6, NKJV). The Hebrew word *hallelu* is an imperative meaning "Praise! Boast!" When you add *Jah*, the name of God, you end up with *hallelujah*, "Praise Jehovah!" (The Greek is *alleluia*.)

Scripture uses *hallelujah* as an expression of rejoicing. The praise in Revelation 19 stands in contrast to the lamentation in Revelation 18, in which the world rulers mourn the fall of Babylon. The heavenly hosts rejoice at the destruction of the harlot and at the marriage of the Lamb. Jesus Christ comes forth to conquer and to establish His righteous kingdom. "Let us be glad and rejoice and give Him glory, for the marriage of the Lamb has come, and His wife has made herself ready" (Rev. 19:7, NKJV).

The heavenly worship so moved the apostle John that he fell at the feet of the angel and started to worship him! I wonder how many of us today would be that stirred by the contemplation of the judgment of the world, the victory of the King of kings, the marriage of the Lamb, and the establishing of the kingdom of God?

In this chapter we have been carefully considering the wonder of God—as Creator, Redeemer, Victorious King, and Conqueror. We have hardly scratched the surface of heaven's praise, and yet our hearts have been stilled and stirred by the wonder of God. The better we know the Word of God, the greater we shall know the God of the Word. Throughout Scripture we find the wonder of God revealed in both declaration and demonstration. "You are the God who does wonders" (Ps. 77:14, NKJV). The God of creation is the God of redemption. He is the king who reigns and the conqueror who defeats every enemy. The better we understand such realities, the better we shall worship Him.

When Queen Victoria had just ascended her throne, she went to hear a performance of *The Messiah*. The court had instructed her that she must not rise when the others stood at the singing of the "Hallelujah Chorus." But when the singers shouted "Hallelujah! Hallelujah! Hallelujah! for the Lord God omnipotent reigneth," she sat on the edge of her chair. Finally, when they came to that part of the chorus that proclaimed Him King of kings, the young queen suddenly rose and stood with bowed head. She later said that though she was the queen, she stood in honor of the King of the whole universe.[3]

THE WONDER OF IT ALL

In October of 2003 Vice President Dick Cheney visited Berrien Springs, Michigan (where I live). Unexpectedly, he went to a local restaurant. There he saw a man at a table by himself, so he went over and sat beside him. The man felt so impressed that Dick Cheney, the vice president of the United States of America, took the time to sit with him and spend a few minutes with him that he said, "I am a Democrat, but I will most likely vote Republican this election."

Now, I want to tell you that Jesus—Jesus Christ of Nazareth, Jesus Christ the Son of God, Jesus Christ the Creator, Jesus Christ the Savior, Jesus Christ the Lord of lords, Jesus Christ the King of kings—thinks that you are so special that He not only took a few minutes of His busy time to talk to you, but He put His life on the line for you.

The Son of God, the ruler of the universe, became a man just because He loves you.

The Son of God, the royal being, died for you just because He loves you.

Jesus Christ, the Savior, loves you so much that He can't be away from you. He sends the Holy Spirit to be with you while He prepares a wonderful heaven for you. And He did all of this just because He loves you.

Jesus Christ, the Redeemer, is coming back soon, just because He loves you.

Jesus Christ lives in your home. Jesus Christ lives in your heart. Jesus Christ lives with you and your family. He is always with you.

The proper response is Wow! Wow! Wonder and worship.

---

[1] Warren W. Wiersbe, *Real Worship: It Will Transform Your Life* (Nashville: Oliver Nelson, 1986), pp. 43-62.

[2] Paul Lee Tan, *Encyclopedia of 7700 Illustrations* (Rockville, Md.: Assurance Publishers, 1979), pp. 549-551, 1340-1342.

[3] Lenya Meitzig and Penny Pierce Rose, *Pathway to God's Treasure* (Wheaton, Ill.: Tyndale House Pub., 2001), p. 40.